WORLD SERIES
HEROES AND GOATS

The Men Who Made History
in America's October Classic

WORLD SERIES HEROES AND GOATS

The Men Who Made History in America's October Classic

BY JOE GERGEN

illustrated with photographs

A ZANDER HOLLANDER
SPORTS BOOK

Random House New York

Library of Congress Cataloging in Publication Data: Gergen, Joe. World Series heroes and goats. (Random House sports library) "A Zander Hollander sports book." SUMMARY: Presents incidents from the World Series from 1905–1981, some representing greatness, and some, "goofs." 1. World Series (Baseball)—History—Juvenile literature. 2. Baseball players—Juvenile literature. [1. World Series (Baseball) 2. Baseball—History. 3. Baseball players] I. Title. II. Series. GV863.A1G47 796.357'782'09 82-611 ISBN: 0-394-85018-1 (pbk.); 0-394-95018-6 (lib. bdg.) AACR2

All the photographs in this book appear courtesy of United Press International with the exception of the following: Clifton Boutelle, page 25; Mitchell B. Reibel, page 2; and Wide World Photos, page 8.

CONTENTS

Contents

INTRODUCTION

As the showcase event in American sports for eight decades, the World Series has meant many things to many players. For some it represented the spring-board to glory. For others it spelled years of shame.

Whatever happens on the baseball field seems larger than life when it happens during a Series. Marvelous catches are charged with greatness, long drives become monumental, and simple errors seem tragic. In baseball sportswriters call a player a goat when he commits a big error in an important game. The heroes whose achievements helped win the championship and the goats whose goofs cost their team a game are all part of the colorful history of the Series.

So it is that after all these years, New York Giant Christy Mathewson's three shutout victories in 1905 stand today alongside New York Yankee George Frazier's three defeats in 1981. One was a hero, one was a goat, yet each has a special place in the World Series story.

Don Larsen is another name one remembers because on an October afternoon in 1956 he pitched a perfect game. And Bill Wambsganss lives on because of one brief moment in the Series of 1920— when he completed an unassisted triple play. They are athletes who shone when their teams most needed it and have been famous ever since.

Players who were already well known have had their greatness proved by heroism in a World Series. That includes such players as Walter Johnson, Grover Cleveland Alexander, Lou Gehrig, Willie Mays, Sandy Koufax, Brooks Robinson, and Roberto Clemente.

The World Series has seen a chain of sluggers stretching in a straight line from Frank Baker, who gave popular expression to the home run in 1911; to Babe Ruth, who called his shot in 1932; to Reggie Jackson, who tied a Ruth record with three home runs in one game in 1977.

And then there were the spectacular mistakes. Fred Snodgrass' mother, following the plays at a newspaper office in Los Angeles, fainted when her son muffed a fly ball in Boston that cost the New York Giants the 1912 Series. And millions cringed when Mickey Owen missed that third strike in 1941. Great players like Ty Cobb and Ted Williams have failed in the Series; and journeymen like Casey Stengel, Dusty Rhodes, and Brian Doyle have risen to unexpected heights.

The World Series gives to all its participants a week or two of importance they never felt before and perhaps never will feel again. Heroes and goats can be made with one pitch, one swing, one groundball, one mighty effort, one dismal slip-up.

They're all here in the stories that follow.

WORLD SERIES
HEROES AND GOATS

The Men Who Made History
in America's October Classic

Rookie Fernando Valenzuela won his first World Series game in 1981.

Stranger Than Fiction

Nobody knew whether there would even be a World Series in 1981. In midsummer the players were on strike and the outlook for a settlement was bleak. But after seven weeks—more than a quarter of the normal season—the umpires' cry of "Play ball" sounded again in the nation's major-league ballparks.

And in October the strangest season of all was capped with an even stranger World Series between the New York Yankees and the Los Angeles Dodgers. They had survived a complicated set of playoffs involving each league's division winners before the strike and after the strike. The team with the best overall won-lost record, the Cincinnati Reds, was actually shut out of the playoffs because it did not win its divisional title in either half of the season.

Perhaps the biggest surprise was that the Series produced a winner at all. After the ceremonial first pitch was thrown at Yankee Stadium on opening night by Joe DiMaggio, the famous Yankee Clipper,

3

the Series turned into a six-game set of surprises, with a flock of heroes and goats.

The Dodgers' Davey Lopes set a record among second basemen with six errors. Their star pitcher, Fernando Valenzuela, only got to pitch in one game. The Yankees gave away one game with dismal outfield play, ran the bases like amateurs, and stranded 55 men, a record for a six-game Series.

Off the field but very much in the action, Yankee owner George Steinbrenner made the headlines daily with detailed criticism of his own players. And as if that wasn't enough, he announced one night that he had punched out two hecklers in an elevator of the Yankees' hotel in Los Angeles.

In keeping with such an atmosphere was the strategy of Bob Lemon. He had taken the place of Gene Michael as manager of the Yankees when Steinbrenner had fired Michael for defying him. Lemon mystified many in the crowd at Yankee Stadium, including his boss, when he lifted starter Tommy John for a pinch-hitter in the fourth inning of game 6 with the score tied, 1–1.

"I can't believe it," John said in the dugout, unaware that he was mouthing the comment to millions of fans watching on television. The impact of Lemon's move became obvious when the Dodgers scored three runs off George Frazier, John's replacement, and went on to score a 9–2 victory for the world championship.

The Yankees, of course, should never have been

in that spot. They won the first two games handily, 5–3 and 3–0, and got Valenzuela in trouble in game 3. But they couldn't knock him out, and he hung on for a 5–4 victory. The next day they played giveaway in the outfield as Reggie Jackson lost a ball in the sun and Bobby Brown misplayed a line drive into a double in what became an 8–7 defeat.

The most dramatic game proved to be game 5, when Dodgers Pedro Guerrero and Steve Yeager hit two homers in a row off Ron Guidry in the seventh inning to turn a 1–0 Yankee lead into a 2–1 Dodger victory. In the eighth inning of that game, Dodger Ron Cey was beaned by a 94-mile-per-hour Rich Gossage fastball. "If he didn't have a helmet on," said a shaken Gossage, "he might be dead."

But Cey was back in the lineup three nights later for game 6 and even delivered the tie-breaking single before suffering dizziness. He shared the Most Valuable Player (MVP) award with Yeager and Guerrero, who had five runs batted in for the game. It marked the first time there was more than one MVP in the Series.

Among the goats there was Dave Winfield, the Yankees' $1.5 million-a-year outfielder, who had a dreadful time at the plate in his first Series, collecting one single in 22 appearances and driving in one run. But the Yankee who will forever be associated with the 1981 Series was George Frazier, a relief pitcher brought up by the Yankees during the season. Frazier was the one whom Lemon called from the bullpen after removing John, and it was Frazier who suffered his third defeat of the Series—although he was the victim more of hard luck than hard hits.

Frazier became only the second pitcher in Series history to lose three games. The other was Claude (Lefty) Williams, one of the eight Black Sox players banned from baseball for throwing the 1919 World Series. "I guarantee you," Frazier said, "I was giving it everything I had."

George Steinbrenner gave his all after the final game in Yankee Stadium. He issued a public apology to the New York fans.

The Tug That Could

Frank Edwin (Tug) McGraw, Jr., gained his nickname early in life from tugging at whatever he was curious about. It served him well when he became a baseball player because from the first moment he set foot on a pitcher's mound, he tugged at the heartstrings of whoever happened to be watching. Like few professional athletes, he had the gift of excitement.

It was no less so in 1980, when he was 36 years old and a member of the Philadelphia Phillies, than it was in 1969, when he won nine games for the Miracle Mets. Or in 1973, when he coined the slogan "You gotta believe" and led the Mets on another furious drive to a National League (NL) pennant. Age had not dampened his enthusiasm for the game he played with such zest.

"I like the feeling I get out there," he explained. "I like the adrenaline flowing. It's a natural high. To look around and see all the people excited, it's just a fun job."

He had done a splendid job in late summer. That,

Philadelphia's Tug McGraw fires away in the opening game of the 1980 World Series against Kansas City.

as much as anything, was the reason the Phillies were in the World Series for the first time since 1950, when they had lost all four games to the Yankees. He had appeared in three of the last four games of the regular 1980 season and in each of the five dramatic games needed to overcome the Houston Astros in the NL playoffs. But there seemed no limit to his energy.

He said he was ready to pitch in the opening game of the Series, and his manager, Dallas Green, took him at his word. Tug McGraw relieved starting pitcher Bob Walk, preserved a 7–6 victory over the Kansas City Royals with two strong innings, and jumped off the mound in celebration. It marked the Phillies' first Series victory since the opening game in 1915, and McGraw treated it like the milestone it was.

McGraw rested during the Phillies' second-game victory but yielded the winning hit in the tenth inning of game 3 to Willie Aikens. The following day Aikens pumped two home runs, his third and fourth of the Series, over the distant fences of Royals Stadium, tying the Series at two games apiece.

It was in the fifth game that McGraw put his stamp on the fall classic. He entered with his team trailing, 3–2, but the Phillies took the lead at 4–3 in the top of the ninth.

McGraw was the center of attention of 42,369 stadium fans and millions more watching on television as he faced the Royals in the bottom of the ninth. He walked Frank White. Then he struck out George Brett, baseball's only .390 hitter. A walk to Aikens brought up designated hitter Hal McRae, who drove McGraw's first pitch deep to left field. After a wait that seemed endless, the ball landed foul and McGraw patted his bursting heart so everyone could see. McRae eventually grounded into a force play but McGraw, pitching carefully, walked Amos Otis. Bases loaded, two out, the game on the line. Tug's time. He responded by striking out Jose Cardenal to give the Phillies a three-to-two edge in games.

Compared to that, the sixth game was a breeze. Relieving Steve Carlton, McGraw worked out of a bases-loaded situation in the eighth and another in the ninth to save a 4–1 victory. What made the final out, an overpowering strikeout of Willie Wilson, strange was the presence of horses, police dogs, and riot patrolmen around the field. They were there to protect the players and to keep the fans from tearing up the field. But they couldn't muffle the cheers for Tug McGraw and the world champion Phillies.

Pittsburgh Pops Concert

The Pittsburgh Pirates called themselves a family. They even had their own anthem—a record by Sister Sledge called "We Are Family" blared from the loudspeakers at every Pirates' game in Three Rivers Stadium. The Pirates danced to it, sang along with it, and lived by it.

Their unifying force, the agreed-on head of the family, was a 38-year-old first baseman with damaged knees. He was Willie Stargell to the outside world, but to the Pirates he was "Pops." "What he means to this club," said Bill Robinson, an outfielder, "words can't describe."

Stargell had spent his entire career with the Pirates. He was a huge but gentle man who never lost his temper, who remained calm in good times and bad, who devoted much of his life to charitable causes. If the Pirates were closer than the players on other major-league teams, it was because of him. "We look at him the way some people pray to whatever god they have," said Dave Parker, the team's most powerful hitter.

Pops had enjoyed greater seasons than 1979 but, considering his age, his performance was remarkable. He batted .281 with 32 home runs and 82 runs batted in, then hit .455 in the National League championship series against the Cincinnati Reds. This would be his second World Series and, most likely, his last.

The start was not encouraging. The Pirates lost the first game and two of the next three. Only three teams in history had overcome a three-to-one deficit to win a World Series.

The Pirates began their comeback in the fifth game with a 7–1 victory in Pittsburgh as Jim Rooker, just a four-game winner during the season but the only rested starter on the team, held the Baltimore Orioles hitless for four innings and limited them to one run in his five innings of work. Then in the sixth game the Pirates evened the Series with a 4–0 victory in Baltimore behind the shutout pitching of John Candelaria and Kent Tekulve. The Series was reduced now to a one-game playoff.

For five innings the Orioles owned game 7 and the championship. Before a joyous crowd of 53,733 in Memorial Stadium which included President Jimmy Carter, Rich Dauer had given Baltimore a 1–0 lead with a third-inning homer. Scott McGregor nursed the lead carefully into the sixth. Then Robinson hit a single that shortstop Kiko Garcia could have fielded but didn't, and the next batter was Stargell. McGregor threw him a fastball thigh-high, on the inside part of the plate, and the crowd gasped.

Stargell's swing sent the ball on a high arc to right field. Ken Singleton ran to the wire fence, leaped as high as he could, and hung there for an instant, his glove arm draped over the mesh. The ball bounced beyond and Stargell finished his tour of the bases. His third home run of the Series sent the Pirates ahead, 2–1, and they won the championship, 4–1, with the help of another outstanding relief performance by Tekulve.

The Pirates couldn't imagine anyone else making the winning hit. "First," Robinson said, "the feeling is that you're elated that you have the lead. Then you realize who hit it and you think it's just so fitting."

The Cinderella Man

He would not have looked out of place in a Boy Scout uniform. Certainly no more out of place than he did in the uniform of the New York Yankees. On a team of established stars and strong personalities, Brian Doyle was a quiet kid along for the ride.

And what a ride it was. Trailing the Boston Red Sox by 14 games in mid-July of 1978, the Yankees had changed managers (Bob Lemon replacing Billy Martin) and rallied to force a one-game playoff for the American League East title. It was enough for Doyle, a 23-year-old infielder who looked too young to shave, that he was on the bench in the major leagues.

His season had been a series of cross-country airplane trips from Tacoma, Washington, site of the Yankees' AAA farm club, to New York and back again. His big-league experience consisted of 52 at-bats. But in the final weekend of the season, All-Star second baseman Willie Randolph suffered a hamstring injury, and suddenly Brian Doyle was in the starting lineup.

14

The Yankees' Brian Doyle, an unlikely batting star, doubles home a run in the sixth game of the 1978 Series. The Dodger catcher is Joe Ferguson.

15

Doyle started in the memorable playoff game at Fenway Park that the Yankees won, 5–4. He started in the American League championship series that the Yankees won in four games against the Kansas City Royals. And he started in the World Series against the Los Angeles Dodgers. And when that was over, not only had Doyle performed flawlessly at second base, but he led all the regulars from both teams in batting, with a .438 average.

"The guy they sent out to replace one of the best ballplayers in the American League played as well as Willie Randolph does," said Dodger outfielder Bill North. "He put the final nails in our coffin."

As was their custom, the Yankees fell behind the Dodgers, losing the first two games. But their defensive skill, especially in the infield, was obvious in the third game as third baseman Graig Nettles made outstanding plays in a 5–1 victory. In game 4 an error charged to Dodger shortstop Bill Russell was the key play in the Yankees' 4–3, 10-inning victory.

It was in the fifth game that Doyle changed from a competent substitute to a star. He singled three times and scored two runs in a 12–2 New York victory. Doyle had seen only one previous World Series, the 1975 classic in which his brother Denny played for the Red Sox, and now Brian himself was a leading man in baseball's greatest drama.

Doyle saved the best for last—game 6. He doubled, singled, and then singled again in his first three appearances in the Yankees' 7–2 clinching victory. Coupled with his singles in his final two at-bats in game 5, he collected five hits in a row, one less than the Series record. His double drove in the first Yankee run and he scored what became the winning run in a three-run second inning. The performances of the eighth and ninth hitters in the Yankee lineup—Doyle and shortstop Bucky Dent, who batted .417—were crucial to New York's success.

But the greatest difference between the teams was not in hitting but in fielding. Dent and Doyle made two difficult and timely double plays in the sixth game, and Doyle saved a run with a sparkling backhanded catch. The Dodgers did nothing out of the ordinary. In two months' time Doyle had gone from minor leaguer to World Series hero. "This is unbelievable," he said. "I feel like Cinderella. I've been to the ball."

A Yankee Hot Dog

Reggie Jackson did not come to New York to be a star. He made that clear the day he signed with the Yankees as a free agent before the 1977 season. "I've brought my star with me," he said then.

And it was the truth. Jackson had already led the American League in home runs and runs batted in while playing for the Oakland A's. He had been the league's Most Valuable Player in 1973. He had starred on three world championship teams. He had done all this with style and swagger, and he was regarded as a "hot dog," a player who liked to show off for the fans. Darold Knowles, an Oakland teammate, once said, "There's not enough mustard in the world to cover Reggie Jackson."

From his first day in training camp, Jackson was an event. The Yankees had reached the World Series in 1976 but had been wiped out in four games by the Cincinnati Reds. Jackson said that never

Reggie Jackson watches the second of his three home runs for the Yankees against the Dodgers in the sixth game of the 1977 World Series.

would happen to a team that he was on. He also said many other things, some of which were not flattering to his new teammates. "I am the straw that stirs the drink," he said in one magazine article. That angered Thurman Munson, the Yankee catcher and team captain.

It was a year of tumult. Manager Billy Martin yanked Jackson from a game at Fenway Park in June, and the two men nearly came to blows in the dugout. Jackson and Munson feuded for a time and then made an uneasy peace. There were few players on the team to whom Jackson was a friend. But in spite of the feeling in the clubhouse, Jackson hit 32 home runs and the Yankees won 100 games and the American League East title.

The American League (AL) championship series was an exhausting five-game struggle against the Kansas City Royals, won by the Yankees in the ninth inning of the final game. Jackson, in a slump, was benched that night by Martin but delivered a key pinch-hit as the Yankees rallied. His manager told him he would be in the lineup for all the World Series games. This was important for a man who liked to be called "Mr. October."

The Yankees and the Dodgers split the first two games of the Series, and the Yankees won the third and fourth games behind Mike Torrez and Ron Guidry. Jackson's slump ended in the fourth game—he doubled to start a three-run inning and then hit a monstrous home run. Although the Yankees lost the fifth game, Jackson homered in his last at-bat in Dodger Stadium.

Dodger pitcher Burt Hooton apparently remembered. He walked Jackson on four pitches in the second inning of the sixth game. In all, Jackson took three swings that night at Yankee Stadium. After each one the ball landed in the stands. He homered off Hooton in the fourth, Elias Sosa in the fifth, and Charlie Hough in the eighth. The three home runs in one Series game tied a mark set by Babe Ruth. The three in a row were a first. Jackson's five home runs in a World Series was another record. "If it were a movie script," said George Steinbrenner, the Yankees' owner, "nobody would believe it."

The Yankees' 8–4 victory earned them their first world championship since 1962, but at the time that seemed less important than Jackson's performance. Steve Garvey, the Dodgers' first baseman, said he was so impressed that he silently applauded into his glove as Jackson rounded the bases for his third home run.

"It's the greatest thing ever in a championship series, an All-Star Game, or a World Series," Garvey said. "The last line in the history books will say, 'Semicolon, the Dodgers and the Yankees also played.'"

For Whom the Bells Toll

It rained. It rained hard on Saturday when the World Series was to continue with the playing of the sixth game in Boston. It rained hard on Sunday. It rained hard again on Monday. What had been a tight 1975 Series soon came down to the daily ritual of commissioner Bowie Kuhn slogging through the Fenway Park outfield, the water oozing into his shoes, and announcing postponement of the game.

There was a general feeling that even when the Boston Red Sox and Cincinnati Reds got back to playing, it wouldn't be the same. The continuity had been lost, it was argued. The anticipation was gone.

How wrong everyone was. It's true that the first five games had their share of excitement. The Red Sox had won the first and fourth games behind their portly pitching wizard, Luis Tiant. The second and third games were so close they weren't settled until the last inning—the Reds winning one in the ninth inning, another game in the tenth with the help of a controversial umpiring decision and two home runs by Tony Perez.

Boston's Carlton Fisk is welcomed home after his game-winning blast tied the 1975 World Series against Cincinnati at three games each.

But all that was just an introduction to the sixth game, which started 79½ hours late and ended the day after it began. It may have been the most fascinating game in Series history. "Isn't this fun?" the Reds' Pete Rose said to Boston catcher Carlton Fisk as he stepped to the plate in the eleventh inning.

There were so many twists and turns. Fred Lynn's home run had given the Red Sox a 3–0 lead in the first inning. Then the Reds tied the score in the fifth and drove the gallant Tiant out of the box with two more runs in the seventh and one in the eighth. That made the score 6–3. The Reds were four outs from a world championship when Boston's Bernie Carbo tied the score with a three-run homer, his second home run of the Series as a pinch-hitter.

The Red Sox loaded the bases with no one out in the ninth but failed to score as George Foster threw out Denny Doyle at the plate after a short fly ball. The Reds threatened in the eleventh, but Fisk made an excellent play to force Rose out at second on a bunt. Then right fielder Dwight Evans made a twisting, leaping catch of a wicked line drive by Joe Morgan, saving the ball from going into the stands and starting a double play.

It wasn't until the twelfth inning, after the clock struck midnight, that the final twist unfolded. The man of the moment was Fisk, the only native New Englander on the Red Sox. Swinging against Pat Darcy, he hit a home run leading off the Boston twelfth, but the sight of it was even greater than the

Pete Rose's all-around play made the difference as the Reds disposed of the Red Sox.

impact. The ball was pulled sharply and appeared to be heading for foul territory. Several steps down the first-base line Fisk began waving and willing it fair with exaggerated body motions. At the instant it struck the foul pole in fair territory, Fisk leaped into the air and bounded around the bases while hundreds of exuberant fans joined him. It was such a gleeful experience that in Charlestown, New Hampshire, where Fisk was raised, a man climbed to the top of an Episcopal church and rang the bells.

"Fisk did what everybody wanted to do, what everybody who jumped out on the field wanted to do," said the Reds' Johnny Bench. "He drove in the winning run in the World Series. He hit a home run. The only thing bigger could be doing that in the seventh game."

Fisk did not hit a homer in the seventh game. Cincinnati's Perez did, a two-run shot after Rose's hard slide had broken up an inning-ending double play and forced a wild throw by second baseman Denny Doyle. It cut the Boston lead to 3–2. Rose singled across the tying run in the seventh. Joe Morgan then singled in the winning run in a 4–3 victory that gave the Reds the world championship.

Rose, who batted .370, was voted the Most Valuable Player of a Series that was rich with heroes. Though the Red Sox had lost the championship, their fans could at least be consoled by Fisk's clutch home run.

Fury at the Plate

They may have been the most unlikely looking collection of athletes ever to appear in a World Series. They wore twenty-first-century uniforms of green and gold and nineteenth-century handlebar mustaches, both inspired by owner Charles O. Finley. They had a mule for a mascot and, it seemed, a fight in the clubhouse every other day.

The Oakland A's weren't taken very seriously by most experts. They had lost their best slugger, Reggie Jackson, to a leg injury in the final game of the playoffs against Detroit. The left-handed side of their fine short-relief pitchers, Darold Knowles, was out of commission. Their opponents in 1972 were the Cincinnati Reds, who had declared themselves the best team in baseball after beating the defending champion Pittsburgh Pirates in the National League playoffs.

It seemed a classic mismatch. And then a semi-regular named Fury Gene Tenace stepped to the plate in Cincinnati's Riverfront Stadium for his first World Series at-bat. He hit a two-run homer. Three innings later he homered again. Never before in baseball history had a man homered in his first two Series appearances. "You can't predict anything in this game," Tenace said. The A's defeated the Reds, 3–2.

Tenace was a surprise even to the A's. He was a man who could play several positions, all of them well enough, none of them terrifically. He had hit only .225, with five home runs, the entire season. During the playoffs he batted .059, and his error at second base cost Oakland the fourth game. His one hit in 17 at-bats drove in the winning run in the fifth game, yet no one expected such an outburst from the A's starting catcher in the World Series.

The fans did expect great things from the other catcher, certainly. The other catcher was Johnny Bench, a leading figure throughout the country and a hero to the fans of Lucasville, Ohio. Lucasville is the river town a hundred miles from Cincinnati where Tenace had grown up in the shadow of the state prison. Even after his two homers, Tenace might not be the most famous man in Lucasville.

In game 2 the Reds were jolted again when Joe Rudi, a competent outfielder who rarely made the headlines, homered and made a stupendous game-saving catch against the wall in a 2–1 Oakland victory. Cincinnati salvaged a 1–0 victory in the third game, but Tenace amazed the Reds again in game 4 with a solo homer and a single in the midst of a game-winning, two-run rally in the ninth. Tenace scored the winning run in the 3–2 victory on Angel Mangual's pinch-hit single.

A three-run homer by Tenace, his fourth of the Series (which equaled a record held by Babe Ruth and Lou Gehrig, among others), was wasted in a 5–4 loss in game 5. In the sixth game the Reds evened the Series with an 8–1 romp back home in Cincinnati, the only game of the Series not decided by one run.

Tenace continued his incredible streak in the deciding seventh game, driving in Oakland's first run with a bad-hop single and doubling across the second run in a 3–2 victory. Allan Lewis, running for Tenace after his sixth-inning double, scored the winning run when center fielder Bobby Tolan collapsed with a hamstring injury while chasing Sal Bando's long drive. Rollie Fingers, appearing in his sixth game, retired Pete Rose with a man on base in the ninth to earn his second save of the Series. The relief ace was also credited with one victory.

The A's scored a total of 16 runs in the seven games and, remarkably, Tenace drove in nine. He batted .348. "He was the biggest factor," said Johnny Bench, his famous counterpart.

Pride of the Pirates

The man had his pride. Perhaps no player in the major leagues had greater pride in his talent and his determination than did Roberto Clemente. What disturbed him was that his ability and his will to play were not fully appreciated.

He was 37 years old as the 1971 season came to a close, and he feared America would never appreciate the way he played baseball. "I want to be remembered for the type of player I am," he said. "I give everything I have according to my ability."

There were no better right fielders in the game, but Clemente got less press coverage than right fielders Hank Aaron, who hit more home runs, and Frank Robinson, who had won MVP awards in both leagues. Pittsburgh also was not a major communications center, and Clemente, an articulate, handsome man, felt slighted by the lack of attention and the absence of offers from corporations to have him sponsor their products. And Clemente suspected prejudice played a part. "I don't see too many idols from Puerto Rico," he said.

The Pirates' Roberto Clemente triples against the Orioles in the sixth game of the 1971 World Series.

For him, the World Series was a chance to educate people, a personal crusade. He had hit a remarkable .341 in his seventeenth major-league season and he continued at that hot pace in the first two games of the 1971 Series against the Baltimore Orioles, singling and doubling in each. But the Pirates were beaten, 5–3 and 11–3.

It took outstanding pitching performances by Steve Blass and Bruce Kison in the third and fourth games to lift the Pirates back into the Series. In game 3 Blass threw a masterful three-hitter, ending Baltimore's 16-game winning streak (including regular-season and American League championship series games). Kison, a 21-year-old sidearmer, allowed only one hit in $6\frac{1}{3}$ innings of relief pitching in the fourth game. That was the first World Series game played at night, and the national television audience was estimated at 61 million. Clemente hit safely in both the 5–1 and 4–3 victories although the big blows were struck by Bob Robertson and Milt May.

Veteran Nelson Briles was the star of the fifth game, blanking the Orioles on two hits and singling in one of the four Pittsburgh runs. Clemente also drove in a run with a single and continued to shine in the field, his speed and the strength of his arm amazing all. "You read about him, you hear about him," said Baltimore third baseman Brooks Robinson, "but in real life he's even better."

The best was yet to come. Clemente tripled and homered in the sixth game, but the Orioles rallied to tie in the seventh inning and won, 3–2, in the tenth. So the next day Clemente homered again in game 7 and the Pirates never lost the lead, winning 2–1 behind Blass's four-hit pitching. For the Series, Clemente batted .414 with two home runs, two doubles, and a triple. "I have peace of mind," he said afterward. "Now everyone knows the way Roberto Clemente plays."

At 37, he had reached the top. He had hit safely in all seven games (after doing the same in his only other World Series, 1960) and earned the MVP award.

Sadly, a year later, after collecting his three-thousandth major-league hit, Clemente died in a plane crash while on a mercy mission from Puerto Rico to earthquake-stricken Nicaragua.

Mr. Gold Glove

He was heavy-legged and slow on the basepaths. His arm wasn't very strong. His retreating hairline made him look older than his 33 years. Yet there were those who considered Brooks Robinson the greatest third baseman ever to play the game.

The 1970 season was the eleventh in a row in which he had won a Gold Glove for his fielding skill. He had made so many "Brooksies" in his career— backhanded stabs behind the bag and diving stops in the hole—that his teammates on the Baltimore Orioles expected every ball hit to the left side of the infield to wind up in his glove. What the World Series offered Robinson was a chance to display his talent in front of a nationwide audience.

And he didn't waste any time. In his first chance in the first game against the Cincinnati Reds, he fielded a grounder hit by Woody Woodward and threw the ball away. The heavily favored Orioles had lost a five-game Series to the Mets the year before, and Robinson's error was a sad way to begin the 1970 Series. But he turned the game around in the

34

The Orioles' Brooks Robinson used the 1970 World Series
against the Reds as a showcase for his brilliant glove work.

sixth inning when he took an apparent double away from Lee May with a dazzling backhanded play, saving at least one run. He then homered in the seventh to break a tie and lift Baltimore to a 4–3 victory.

Robinson caused more gasps in the second game when, with his team trailing, 4–0, and the Cincinnati Reds threatening to break open the game, he gloved another hot smash by May and turned it into a double play. Then he singled across a run in the midst of the Orioles' five-run fifth-inning rally. Baltimore won, 6–5. "He beat us two days in a row with his fielding," said Cincinnati manager Sparky Anderson. "Without Robinson, it would be 2–0 the other way."

The Orioles won the third game easily, 9–3, as Brooks Robinson doubled twice, Frank Robinson homered, and pitcher Dave McNally hit a grand slam. What dazzled the Reds, though, were three more defensive gems by the third baseman. He made a leaping grab of Tony Perez's hopper in the first, starting a double play. Robinson threw out Tommy Helms on a tricky slow roller in the second inning, then made a diving stab of Johnny Bench's line drive in the sixth. "He could play third base," said the Reds' Pete Rose in admiration, "with a pair of pliers."

Although the Reds did manage to save game 4, 6–5, it was through no fault of Robinson's, who went 4-for-4 at bat, including a home run. Cincinnati jumped to a 3–0 lead in the fifth game, but

Frank Robinson's two-run homer in the bottom of the first chilled the Reds, and the Orioles bombarded the sore-armed Jim Merritt in the second. The outcome was settled early. All that remained was the finishing touch, a final tip of the glove by Brooks Robinson.

It came in the ninth inning of the Orioles' 9–3 victory. Bench, the lead-off batter, drilled a line drive over third base that appeared headed for foul territory. Fair or foul, it didn't matter. Robinson dove across the line and speared it anyway. Fittingly, the last out of the game was a groundball to the third baseman. Robinson had hit .429 with six runs batted in, but what impressed the Reds was his fielding.

"Nobody on our team anticipated hitting the ball as well as we did and not coming up with anything," Bench said. "I can't hit it outside him. Hit it twenty feet in and he dives and gets it."

The Amazin' Mets

People called it a miracle that the Mets were in a World Series. The Miracle Mets, that's the name they earned after seven years of abuse by rising from ninth place in 1968 to a National League pennant in 1969. God, pitching star Tom Seaver decided, had an apartment in New York that season.

It was the year that mankind took one giant step on the moon. Many thought the Mets' accomplishment was more amazing. In one season they had reached .500 for the first time, been to first place, won the Eastern Division, and swept the Atlanta Braves in the first National League championship series. Seven years after setting the saddest of records—120 losses in 160 games—they won 100 games and the admiration of millions.

Still, in 1969 they were decided underdogs against a great Baltimore team that had won 109 games in the American League. When the Orioles defeated 25-game winner Tom Seaver in the Series opener, it seemed the miracle had run its course. But in game 2 Jerry Koosman, a 25-year-old left-hander in his second full major-league season, dueled Dave McNally to a 1–1 standstill through eight innings. The Mets evened the Series at one game apiece when Ed Charles, Jerry Grote, and Al Weis stroked three two-out singles in a row in the ninth.

Weis was one of the quieter members of what was mainly a young, brash team. He was a 31-year-old often traded infielder who still wore a crewcut and hardly ever said a word. Manager Gil Hodges used him at shortstop and second base during the season, and although Weis batted only .215, he was a part-time player at second base with left-handed hitter Ken Boswell in the playoffs and the Series. "I don't say much," he said, "but I play the game hard in my own way."

Game 3, the first Series contest ever played in New York's Shea Stadium, belonged to Tommie Agee, the center fielder who had come to the Mets the previous year from the Chicago White Sox in a package that included Weis. Agee homered to lead off the bottom of the first inning. He then made spectacular catches with two runners on in the fourth and the bases loaded in the seventh to preserve a 5–0 victory behind hard-throwing youngsters Gary Gentry and Nolan Ryan.

It was another mystifying catch, this a backhanded diving stab by right fielder Ron Swoboda in the ninth, that checked the Orioles in game 4. The Mets broke a 1–1 tie in the tenth when J. C. Martin, trying to bunt two base runners home, was struck in the left wrist by pitcher Pete Richert's throw to first base. Pinch-runner Rod Gaspar scored from second base as the ball rolled into right field.

That brought the unbelievable Mets to a 3–1 lead in the Series and they barreled ahead in remarkable fashion. In game 5, trailing, 3–0, after three innings, Koosman shut down the Orioles by allowing only one hit over the final six innings. New York cut the lead to a single run when Donn Clendenon clubbed a two-run homer in the sixth after Cleon Jones reached first as a result of being hit on the shoe by a McNally pitch. Then, in the seventh, the unlikely Weis homered to tie the score at 3–3. Doubles by Jones and Swoboda and two Baltimore errors gave the Mets a 5–3 lead in the eighth.

As Dave Johnson's fly ball fell into Jones's glove for the final out in the top of the ninth, a blizzard of paper, ticker tape, and computer punch cards rained down from New York skyscrapers. The weather bureau described conditions as "cloudy with falling confetti." The Mets had done it, by God.

And Al Weis, the slender glove man, had become a hero. Even though he had hit only six home runs in his entire career before the Series, it was his homer that had made the final victory possible. And the substitute had batted .455 with five hits, four walks, and a sacrifice fly.

Tiger on the Mound

When he was two, Mickey Lolich suddenly became a left-hander. He did this by riding his tricycle over the curb into a parked motorcycle, which landed on top of him. The doctor had him exercise his left arm (he had broken his left collarbone) to strengthen it—and the world had another southpaw.

Not many people outside Detroit were aware of that fact when the 1968 World Series got under way. Then again, not many people outside Detroit were aware of Mickey Lolich. He was the "other" pitcher on the Tigers, the one who had never won 20 games, let alone 30. Denny McLain was the acknowledged star of the staff after a 31–6 season, baseball's first 30-game winner in 30 years.

McLain, of course, drew the first-game assignment. He also drew Bob Gibson as an opponent. Gibson had won three games for the St. Louis Cardinals in the 1967 Series and was coming off a 22-9 season in which he set a National League record for the lowest earned-run average over 300 or more innings, 1.12 per game. The match-up was no contest

41

as Gibson overpowered the Tigers, 4–0, striking out 17 for a Series one-game record.

It fell to Lolich to even matters the next day. Lolich looked like anything but a model—he wore his belt very low to give his pot belly room to breathe—but he set down the Cards, 8–1, on six hits. "Sometimes I hate my ancestors," he said, commenting on his build. "All the men had bodies like this."

The Cards recovered to win the third and fourth games in Detroit, Gibson again besting McLain to give St. Louis a commanding three-games-to-one margin. It might have ended the next day when the Cards carried a 3–2 lead into the seventh inning. But Al Kaline, appearing in his first Series after a magnificent 16-year career, singled with the bases loaded as the Tigers rallied for a 5–3 victory behind Lolich. Kaline had been injured part of the season and was in the starting lineup only because manager Mayo Smith had moved his regular center fielder, Mickey Stanley, to shortstop, making room for the future Hall of Famer.

In a second gamble Smith chose the arm-weary McLain to start the sixth game and this time he coasted to a 13–1 victory. That left Lolich to oppose Gibson in the seventh game on only two days' rest. "I'm hoping for six good innings," Smith said. He got more than he expected.

Hefty Mickey Lolich of Detroit readies a pitch in one of his three victories against St. Louis in the 1968 World Series.

The game was scoreless after six innings. But in the seventh, with two out and two runners on base, Detroit's Jim Northrup hit a rising line drive to center field. Curt Flood, the best at his position in the National League, broke in, realized his mistake, and attempted to change direction. He stumbled. By the time he recovered, the ball had sailed over his head for a triple, the first two runs scoring in a 4–1 victory that gave the Tigers the world championship and Lolich his third triumph.

"First of all, I didn't see the ball off the bat," said Flood, the goat of the Series. "That crowd . . . all those [white] shirts . . . Then I slipped. Ah, I screwed it up. I don't want to make any alibis about it. I lost it."

The Tigers had many heroes, including Stanley, who handled 31 out of 33 chances at shortstop, and Kaline, who batted .379 with two home runs and eight runs batted in. But there was no hero bigger than Lolich, and not just because of his shape. "I'm just not the hero type," he said when it was over. "The hero of the Tigers has never been Mickey Lolich. It's always been Al Kaline or the guy who won thirty-one games."

But this time it was Mickey.

An Impossible Dream

This was the kind of year it was: At the start of the season Elston Howard of the New York Yankees delivered a two-out, ninth-inning single to break up a no-hit bid by Boston rookie Billy Rohr and received hate mail from Red Sox fans. By the end of the season Rohr was in the minor leagues and Howard was receiving ovations in Fenway Park for his part in what was called the Impossible Dream.

After a ninth-place finish the year before, the Red Sox had struggled through a wild American League pennant race and clinched the flag on the last day of the 1967 season. Their stars had been Carl Yastrzemski, an outfielder who had enjoyed a Triple Crown season, and Jim Lonborg, a right-handed pitcher who had won 22 games. Among the indispensable people had been Howard, a frequent All-Star catcher with the Yankees who had been bought by the Red Sox in August to provide leadership at that position.

Howard was 38 years old and his arm had weakened. He had trouble throwing out swift base run-

Lou Brock of the Cardinals slides across the plate in the sixth game of the 1967 World Series. The Red Sox's Elston Howard is too late with the tag.

ners. The St. Louis Cardinals, it so happened, had just such a base runner. Lou Brock had led the National League in stolen bases for the second year in a row. He wasted no time in testing Howard. Brock singled on the third pitch of the first game and stole second on the fourth. After his third of four hits, he again stole second in the seventh inning and scored on two infield outs. It was the winning run in Bob Gibson's 2–1 victory.

Lonborg and Yastrzemski evened the Series the following day, Lonborg pitching a brilliant one-hitter and Yaz homering twice in a 5–0 triumph. Back in St. Louis, the Cards won the third and fourth games as Brock doubled, tripled, singled twice, stole a base, and scored three runs.

Gibson was the winning pitcher in game 4, tossing a five-hit shutout. Again it was up to Lonborg, and this time he responded with a three-hitter in a 3–1 victory.

In spite of a home run, single, and stolen base by Brock in game 6 at Fenway, the Red Sox won, 8–4, with a four-run rally in the seventh. The Cards had a strong Gibson, fully recovered from a broken leg suffered during the season, ready for the seventh game. Lonborg started for the Red Sox with only two days' rest.

It was no contest. The Cards roared to leads of 4–0 and 7–1 before manager Dick Williams removed the courageous but exhausted Lonborg. Gibson homered for one run and Brock manufactured another, singling, stealing second and third, and scoring on a sacrifice fly by Roger Maris. Gibson went the distance, allowing only three hits in a 7–2 triumph.

The gold-plated hero of the Series, however, was Brock, who went on to break the one-season and career records for stolen bases. Yastrzemski, the Boston left fielder, also had a wonderful Series, batting .400 with three homers. Brock, the St. Louis left fielder, had a better one. Not only did he lead both clubs in batting with a .414 mark, but he stole seven bases in seven attempts, a Series record, and scored eight runs. "I was just playing my game," he said.

The game was never so breathtaking.

Lost in the Sun

Pitching and defense were the ingredients that made the Los Angeles Dodgers the overwhelming favorite to win the 1966 World Series. They didn't have high batting averages or score many runs, but they had won two of the three previous Series with virtually the same cast. Best of all, they had Sandy Koufax.

Koufax was the dominant pitcher in baseball. According to some experts, he was the finest pitcher in two generations. At the age of 30, he had pitched four no-hitters, including a perfect game, and had led the National League in earned-run average for five seasons in a row. In typical style he had pitched the Dodgers to the 1966 NL pennant on the final day of the season, raising his record to 27–9.

Because of that last game, Koufax surrendered the first-game Series assignment against the Baltimore Orioles to Don Drysdale, the other half of baseball's most effective pitching duo. Participating in their first Series, the Orioles were a hard-hitting team led by Frank and Brooks Robinson. But their pitching staff was unreliable because of its youth and inexperience.

Dave McNally, a 23-year-old left-hander, seemed to justify the fears of Baltimore fans when, after being staked to a 4–0 lead courtesy of home runs by both Robinsons, he yielded a homer to Jim Lefebvre in the second inning and then lost all control in the third, walking three to load the bases. Manager Hank Bauer called for Moe Drabowsky, a fun-loving veteran who had played 10 years in the majors without distinction.

In the next 6⅔ innings Drabowsky justified his entire career. He limited the Dodgers to one base hit while striking out 11, and the Orioles won, 5–2. Still, the Dodgers were not upset. They had Koufax, the great equalizer, going in game 2. What they did not have, though, was their usual steady defense.

Jim Palmer, a 20-year-old right-hander, battled Koufax evenly through four innings. In the fifth it happened. With one on and one out, Paul Blair hit a drive to center. Willie Davis, perhaps the fastest man in baseball, got to it quickly but lost it in the glare of an uncommonly bright sun. It fell at his feet, and Baltimore had runners at second and third.

Bearing down, Koufax got Andy Etchebarren to fly weakly toward Davis. As the center fielder ranged in, he again lost the ball in the sun. It glanced off his glove, and in haste and frustration he threw the ball past third base. Two runs scored and Etchebarren wound up on third, from where he scored on Luis Aparicio's double. Davis had become the first player in Series history to commit three errors in one inning.

"The ball hit by Blair got into a certain spot in the sun coming down and I couldn't see it," Davis said. "The second time, I waved my arms to show I had lost the ball, but I was closest to it and I made a stab for the ball. I guess I made the throwing error after dropping the ball because I was mad at myself and embarrassed. That was the worst thing that ever happened to me."

And to the Dodgers as well. They never recovered, losing the second game, 6–0. Blair's home run was the only run in the third game. Frank Robinson homered for a 1–0 victory in the fourth game, Wally Bunker and McNally pitching complete-game shutouts to complete the startling sweep. Told by their scouts to challenge Dodger batters with fastballs, the Orioles held Los Angeles scoreless for the last 33 innings and limited the NL champs to a .142 batting average, the lowest in Series history.

Davis' role as goat was confirmed for life when, a month after the Series, Koufax announced his retirement because of an arthritic elbow. His final major-league game had been lost in the sun.

A Star Is Born

The 1964 World Series marked the rise of one star and the fall of another. It was the first chance for Bob Gibson to gain national attention and the final chance for Whitey Ford, the most successful of all Series pitchers. And it also marked the end of a dynasty, the last stand of the great Yankee teams assembled by general manager George Weiss.

Ford, whose 10 victories were a Series record, started the first game for the Yankees against the St. Louis Cardinals and was blasted, 9–5. Hampered by various arm ailments, Ford did not pitch again in this or any other Series.

Gibson's first Series start the following day was no more rewarding. He was charged with four runs in eight innings and the Yankees won routinely, 8–3, behind rookie sensation Mel Stottlemyre. In the ninth inning of that game, relief pitcher Barney Schultz, who had earned a save in the first game,

Hard-throwing Cardinal Bob Gibson struck out 31 Yankees and won two games in the 1964 Series.

was rocked for a home run by the normally light-hitting Phil Linz.

Schultz was a veteran knuckleball pitcher who had appeared in the uniforms of 16 minor- and major-league teams in a career that was long but undistinguished. His only success story had been brilliant pitching down the stretch as the Cardinals overtook the faltering Philadelphia Phillies to win the National League pennant. But the glow faded with the Series. In the third game he was summoned in the ninth inning with the score tied, 1–1. His first pitch to Mickey Mantle landed in the stands for a game-winning homer. Later Schultz sagged on a clubhouse stool and cried.

As suddenly as the Series had shifted to the Yankees, though, it quickly went back into the hands of the Cards. St. Louis third baseman Ken Boyer, playing the same position as his brother Clete did for the Yankees, hit a grand-slam homer off Al Downing in the sixth inning of game 4 to turn a 3–0 deficit into a 4–3 victory.

Now it was Gibson's turn, and the intensely competitive, hard-throwing right-hander did not disappoint. Gibson outdueled Stottlemyre in the fifth game, 5–2, on Tim McCarver's home run in the tenth inning.

The Yankees won the sixth game, 8–3, leaving managers Yogi Berra of the Yankees and Johnny Keane of the Cards with an important decision: Go with a rested pitcher or their best on two days' rest?

Both of them chose the latter course. In game 7 the Cards drove out Stottlemyre after four innings and held leads of 6–0 and 7–3. Gibson was an exhausted pitcher in the ninth, but Keane stuck with him even after homers by Clete Boyer and Linz had cut the margin to 7–5. "I made a commitment," Keane would later explain, "to his heart." With his last ounce of energy Gibson justified that commitment by retiring Bobby Richardson on a pop fly. Richardson had set a Series record by collecting 13 hits.

On the day after the seventh game Berra was fired and Keane resigned. Within four days Keane was named Yankee manager in one of the oddest turnabouts in baseball history.

Sandy's Series

They took the Dodgers out of Brooklyn following the 1957 season, but they couldn't take Brooklyn out of the Dodgers. When the most-spirited of World Series rivalries—between the Yankees and the Dodgers—continued in 1963 after a seven-year break, the Dodgers called Los Angeles home. But it was one of Brooklyn's own who led them against the Yankees.

His name was Sandy Koufax and he was a left-handed pitcher whose few appearances in hometown Ebbets Field had been ruined by wildness. Growing to maturity in Los Angeles, he had become the finest pitcher in baseball.

Matched against Whitey Ford in the opening game at Yankee Stadium, Koufax gave a stunning performance. He struck out the first five batters he faced and completed a 5–2 Dodger victory by fanning pinch-hitter Harry Bright for his fifteenth strikeout, bettering by one the record for a Series game set by former Dodger Carl Erskine.

The New York crowd of 69,000 was so absorbed

56

Sandy Koufax of the Dodgers set the tone for the 1963 World
Series when he struck out the first five Yankees in game 1.

by Koufax's effort that it actually cheered for the Dodger to strike out the Yankees in the ninth. "I wait all these years to get into a World Series," Bright said, "and when I do, sixty thousand people root for me to strike out."

Dodger John Roseboro hit the big blow of the game, a three-run homer, and Bill Skowron, traded by the Yankees the previous winter, drove in two runs with a pair of singles. Skowron also had a gratifying day in game 2, homering for an insurance run in a 4–1 Dodger victory. The winning pitcher was Johnny Podres, who eight years earlier had been the hero of Brooklyn's only world championship.

By game 3 it was obvious that Dodger pitching was too powerful for the Yankees. Don Drysdale hurled a four-hitter and bested Jim Bouton, 1–0. All the Yankees had to look forward to in the fourth game was a rematch with Koufax, who had sent them into a slump in the opener.

Koufax wasn't as overpowering in game 4 as he had been in game 1, but he was sharp enough. Only Mickey Mantle's home run in the seventh marred his afternoon's work. The Dodgers had scored first on Frank Howard's mammoth homer into the second deck of Dodger Stadium in the fifth inning. Los Angeles broke the 1–1 tie against the unlucky Ford in the seventh when first baseman Joe Pepitone lost Clete Boyer's throw against a background of white shirts, allowing Jim Gilliam to reach third and score on Willie Davis' sacrifice fly.

The Dodgers managed only two hits in the game, both by Howard, but still closed out the first Series sweep ever registered against the Yankees. Koufax's two victories marked him as someone special, a status he would justify with four no-hit games before an elbow injury cut short his career in 1966.

From Goat to Hero

The 1962 World Series proved that baseball is a game of inches. Also that yesterday's goat can be tomorrow's hero. The first coast-to-coast world championship, featuring the Yankees and the San Francisco Giants, formed the backdrop for one of the most ironic moments in the history of the event.

There was little to choose between the teams as they battled through six games and a stretch of weather that would have dampened Noah's spirits. There was one rainout in New York and three postponements in a row in San Francisco. With open dates for travel, it was 13 days between the opener and the climactic seventh game in San Francisco's Candlestick Park.

It was down to one game, winner-take-all, when Ralph Terry of the Yankees opposed Jack Sanford of the Giants in a battle of 20-game winners. Only two years earlier Terry had thrown the pitch that Bill Mazeroski hit for the Series-winning homer in the ninth inning of the seventh game. Few men get two chances.

60

Terry did the most with his opportunity. Staked to a 1–0 lead in the fifth inning when Tony Kubek grounded into a bases-loaded double play with none out, Terry allowed only two hits through the first eight innings. And he seemed to have the game in his grasp when he struck out Felipe Alou and Chuck Hiller following Matty Alou's bunt single in the ninth.

At that point, though, Willie Mays lined a ball down the right-field line for a double. Shackled for much of the Series, Mays had visions of a game-tying triple. But right fielder Roger Maris made an excellent play in the corner and Bobby Richardson a strong throw home, holding Matty Alou at third. The next batter was the dangerous Willie McCovey, with the Series on the line. Terry had been there before.

First base was open; a left-handed hitter was at bat. Manager Ralph Houk made his way to the mound. "Here's this big ex-army major, right?" Terry said. "So he stands there shaking and says, 'I don't know what the hell I'm doing out here. I don't know what to say.' I didn't want to throw a strike to Willie McCovey. I wanted to work on him with first base open."

What happened then was a lucky accident. The first pitch was inside, and McCovey pulled it foul. The second pitch McCovey took for ball one.

But the third pitch was a fastball over the plate. McCovey swung, there was a loud crack, and a white blur rushed toward right field. But at the moment the Giants and their fans began leaping to their feet in anticipation of victory, Yankee second baseman Bobby Richardson lifted his glove and intercepted the ball.

The Yankees had won the Series, and Terry had gone from goat in 1960 to hero in 1962. "If it had been a foot higher or two feet either left or right," McCovey said sadly, "I would have been a hero."

Mighty Maz

It didn't make sense. The Yankees had outscored the Pittsburgh Pirates, 46–17, had set a string of batting records, and yet were being asked to play a seventh game for the 1960 world championship. If it had been a prizefight, either the Pittsburgh corner would have thrown in the towel or the referee would have been forced to stop it.

But this was baseball, and the Pirates had managed to stay even in a very one-sided Series by squeezing out three narrow victories behind the clutch relief pitching of Elroy Face. In the arithmetic of the game, the Pirates' wins counted just as much as the Yankees' 16–3, 12–0, and 10–0 triumphs. Still, it seemed only a matter of nine innings before the Yankees would prove beyond a doubt that they were the best team in the sport.

After 7½ innings it seemed a certainty. The Yankees had rallied from a 4–0 deficit to take a 7–4 lead against Pittsburgh ace Vernon Law and the gritty Face. Six outs remained for the Pirates. And then a pebble took its place in Series history.

Pittsburgh's Gino Cimoli was on first with a pinch-hit single in the eighth inning when Bill Virdon hit a groundball toward shortstop Tony Kubek. A perfect double-play ball. But as the shortstop reached down for the ball, it struck a pebble and took an unexpected hop, hitting Kubek in the throat. Kubek had to be taken to a hospital, and the Pirates took the opportunity to score five runs, the last three on Hal Smith's homer. Now the Pirates led, 9–7.

The mighty Yankees were down to their last three outs. But once again Pittsburgh pitching wasn't equal to the task. The Yankees scored two runs off Bob Friend in the ninth to tie the score at 9–9. Ralph Terry, the losing starter in game 4, was called from the bullpen. He was the Yankees' fifth pitcher of the game.

Bill Mazeroski was the lead-off batter. He was a 24-year-old second baseman who was a marvel with the glove but was not regarded as a deep threat in spite of his homer in game 1. After all, he was the eighth hitter in the lineup.

"I'd been up in the seventh inning with a runner on and one out and I tried too hard," Mazeroski said. "I wasn't after a home run then but I did want to hit the ball hard, and I overswung and hit into a double play. In the ninth I really did want to hit a home run but I remembered that double play and reminded myself not to overswing."

With a count of 1-0, Maz took a relaxed swing,

and the ball shot off the bat toward the left-field wall in Forbes Field. Yogi Berra took one step back, then stopped and watched it sail over the wall. Rounding first, Maz suddenly leaped high, waved his arms, and swung his cap in the air. He was mobbed by teammates and fans alike as he came home after one of the most dramatic homers in Series history. The Pirates had won, 10–9.

The people of Pittsburgh reacted to the Pirates' first world championship in 35 years with total abandon. They staged impromptu parades and parties in the downtown streets so that the police were forced to turn back motorists. The Yankees, who batted a record .338, were stunned by their defeat, none more so than Terry, who had thrown only two pitches. What kind of pitch did Maz hit? "The wrong one," Terry said.

Goose Eggs

In 1948, when the Braves had won their last National League pennant and still represented the city of Boston, the team's two leading pitchers were Warren Spahn and Johnny Sain. In 1957, when the Braves faced the New York Yankees in the World Series, the Braves' home was Milwaukee. But Spahn was still the ace of the staff, and the number 2 pitcher was Lew Burdette.

Burdette was a lean right-hander from the village of Nitro, West Virginia, whose reputation was tainted. According to opposing hitters, Burdette threw an illegal spitball. The Yankees knew all about the charges. Burdette had been with their organization before being traded to the Braves in 1951 for, of all people, Johnny Sain.

It was Spahn, the 21-game winner, who received the starting assignment in the first game, but he was no match for Whitey Ford and the Yankees, losing 3–1.

Burdette, a 17-game winner during the regular season, got the Braves even by besting Bobby

66

Shantz in game 2 by the score of 4–2. He held the Yankees scoreless over the final six innings and then shut them out, 1–0, in the fifth game.

That victory enabled the Braves to take a three-to-two edge in games, a 12–3 rout by the Yankees in game 3 having been offset by a 7–5 Milwaukee triumph in 10 innings in game 4. It was in the fourth game that the celebrated shoe polish incident happened. It may have been the turning point of the entire Series.

The Yankees had rallied from a 4–1 deficit to tie the score on Elston Howard's three-run homer with two out in the ninth. They went ahead, 5–4, on Hank Bauer's run-scoring triple in the tenth off Spahn. But Nippy Jones, batting for Spahn in the bottom of the tenth at Milwaukee's County Stadium, was hit on the foot by a Tommy Byrne pitch. Home-plate umpire Augie Donatelli called the pitch a ball, but Jones got back the ball and showed it to Donatelli. On it was a telltale black smudge. It looked like shoe polish. The umpire, agreeing that the pitch had indeed hit Jones on the foot, awarded him first base. The Braves went on to score three runs on a double by Johnny Logan and a homer by Eddie Mathews off Bob Grim.

Hank Bauer's seventh-inning homer lifted the Yankees to a 3–2 victory in game 6 back at Yankee Stadium. It was Spahn's turn in the rotation for the seventh game but the left-hander came down with the flu. Manager Fred Haney sent Burdette to the mound with only two days' rest.

It had been 11 years since a pitcher won three games in a Series, 37 years since a pitcher had started and finished three winning games. Burdette did both in game 7 with a seven-hit effort, sailing to a 5–0 victory and running his scoreless mark to 24 innings. Only Christy Mathewson's three shutouts in a row in 1905 stands as a greater pitching achievement in World Series history.

The Perfect Game

He was a big jug-eared man who threw the ball hard but with only moderate success. Until, that is, the fifth game of the 1956 World Series.

In 52 previous World Series no one had earned the right to be called perfect. And then along came New York's Don Larsen.

The Series, the last one to match the Yankees and the Brooklyn Dodgers, was tied at two games apiece when Larsen walked to the mound at Yankee Stadium. He had been battered by the Dodgers in game 2, lasting just 1⅔ innings. Certainly there was nothing in his background to suggest greatness. Two years earlier, while with the Baltimore Orioles, he had lost more games (21) than any other pitcher in the American League. He had won 11 games for the Yankees in 1956 but had managed to finish only six starts.

Larsen's opponent, Sal Maglie, had enjoyed a remarkable comeback season at the age of 39 after being traded to the Dodgers from their archrivals, the New York Giants. And Maglie had checked the

The scoreboard tells the story as the Yankees' Don Larsen fires the final pitch against the Dodgers in game 5 of the 1956 World Series.

Yankees in the first game. This game would mark the turning point of the Series.

Maglie was tough through the first six innings, allowing one run on Mickey Mantle's home run in the fourth and a second on Hank Bauer's single in the sixth. Larsen, however, was unhittable. With the help of a superb play by shortstop Gil McDougald on a deflection off third baseman Andy Carey's glove in the second inning and Mantle's backhanded running grab of Gil Hodges' drive to left center in the fifth, Larsen set down the first 18 Dodgers. Larsen, with one exception (Pee Wee Reese in the first inning), had never gone to more than a two-ball count on a batter.

The no-windup delivery he had turned to late in the season in order to improve his control seemed to baffle the Dodgers in the October shadows. He was throwing easily, effortlessly, but the ball was exploding at the plate.

By the seventh inning the players and the 64,519 spectators alike were beginning to feel the tension. Three Dodgers up, three Dodgers down. There was one anxious moment in the eighth, but Carey lunged to grab Hodges' liner and the Dodgers again went out in order.

"I was so weak in the knees out there in the ninth inning," Larsen said, "I thought I was going to faint." Carl Furillo, the first batter, fouled off four pitches, then flied to right. The crowd uttered a collective gasp as Roy Campanella hit a long drive to

71

left. The ball hooked foul and Campy then grounded out.

Brooklyn was down to its last out. Larsen was one batter away from the first no-hitter in Series history, the first perfect game anywhere since Charles Robertson of the Chicago White Sox threw one against the Detroit Tigers on April 30, 1922. Dale Mitchell was the pinch-hitter for Maglie. "When Mitchell came up," Larsen said, "I was so nervous I almost fell down. My legs were rubbery and my fingers didn't feel like they were on my hand. I said to myself, 'Please help me out, somebody.' "

Help wasn't necessary. Mitchell fell behind on the count, 1-2, fouled off one pitch, and then took a fastball on the outside corner. Babe Pinelli, umpiring his last big-league game, raised his right hand for strike three. It was a perfect game!

The Dodgers battled back to win the sixth game at Ebbets Field, 1–0, as Clem Labine outdueled Bob Turley in 10 innings. But there was no stopping the Yankees in game 7. Berra hit two home runs off Don Newcombe, and Johnny Kucks pitched a three-hitter in a 9–0 rout.

But for all who were there or who watched on television, the real climax of the Series had happened on October 8 when Berra leaped into the arms of Larsen seconds after Larsen had vaulted into the history books.

A First in Brooklyn

Twice before, the Brooklyn Dodgers had been in a similar position. Twice before, they had faltered in the seventh game of a World Series. No matter how good their team was, there was little reason in 1955 for the Flatbush Faithful to believe they were on the verge of their first world championship.

The opponents were the New York Yankees, and that was not good news. The Yankees had defeated the Dodgers in the seventh game in 1947 and 1952. They had also beaten the Brooks in five-game Series in 1941 and 1949 and a six-game Series in 1953. In the borough of Brooklyn, it seemed, the Yankees lived to torment the Dodgers.

No team in Series history had won a championship after losing the first two games, as the 1955 Dodgers had done. They had swept the middle three games played at Ebbets Field, thanks largely to the slugging of Duke Snider, but were humbled in game 6 at Yankee Stadium by Whitey Ford, 5–1.

Already Dodger fans were consoling themselves with the expression, "Wait 'til next year." The seventh game would be played in Yankee Stadium, a Dodger graveyard, and Brooklyn's starting pitcher was a 23-year-old who didn't throw very hard. Poor Johnny Podres. Poor Dodgers.

Although Podres had only a 9–10 record during the regular season, he had beaten the Yankees in game 3, 8–3. And he had a plan, to throw a lot of changeups and breaking balls early in the game and then switch to fastballs when the late-afternoon shadows made the ball difficult for the batter to follow.

In spite of all his plans, it was a substitution by manager Walter Alston that ultimately frustrated the Yanks. The Dodgers were leading, 2–0, on Gil Hodges' fourth-inning single and sixth-inning sacrifice fly when Alston removed second baseman Don Zimmer, shifted Jim Gilliam from left field to second, and inserted a fleet-footed Cuban named Sandy Amoros in left field to improve the defense.

Billy Martin, the Yankee lead-off batter in the sixth, walked, and Gil McDougald was safe on a bunt. Yogi Berra, a powerful left-handed hitter, was next. Amoros was moved toward left-center. When Berra sliced a drive toward the left-field corner, it seemed certain to be a double or even a triple. Martin and McDougald were running with the sound of the bat and were about to score easily. But Amoros, racing across the field, stuck out his glove and made a remarkable catch at full gallop. He threw to shortstop Pee Wee Reese, who easily doubled McDougald at first with a relay to Hodges.

Still confident, Podres blew down the Yankees over the final three innings, and Brooklyn had its first championship. Also its last. The famous franchise was moved to Los Angeles after the 1957 season. "I was lucky," Podres said, "but I was damn good, too."

Dusty and the Indians

That they played baseball in the Polo Grounds was a source of both amazement and amusement to many. Of all the historic ballparks in America, it was the most gloriously misshapen relic. John McGraw's Giants had started out there and the Yankees had played there as well, until Babe Ruth's popularity created the need for a larger stadium for the Yanks across the Harlem River in the Bronx.

Playing baseball in the Polo Grounds was like playing stickball on a New York street, with left field and right field as close as the row houses on either side and center field as distant as the far end of the block.

Into such a tunnel of tradition in 1954 strode the Cleveland Indians, fresh from the most successful season in American League history. The Indians had won an AL record 111 games thanks to a superb pitching staff boasting 20-game winners Bob Lemon and Early Wynn, workhorse Mike Garcia, and the legendary Bob Feller. Al Rosen, Larry Doby, and Vic Wertz provided raw hitting power, and second base-

76

man Bobby Avila was the league batting champion. So the Indians were heavily favored to defeat the Giants.

What few experts had reckoned with, though, was how the Polo Grounds would affect the outcome. If ever a World Series depended on the first game, it was the 1954 classic. In the eighth inning of game 1, with the score tied at 2–2, Wertz hit a monstrous drive to center field. Two base runners were off and running with the sound of the blast. So, too, was Willie Mays, the Giants' incredible center fielder.

All that was visible from home plate was his number, 24. He turned immediately to face the bleachers, tracking the ball over his shoulder as he ran farther and farther until he was almost at the base of the stands. Then he reached up like a football receiver and caught the ball, 460 feet from home plate. With a whirl and a throw, he prevented a runner from scoring and the game went into extra innings.

If the Indians were discouraged by the catch, they were demoralized by Dusty Rhodes's game-winning hit in the tenth. There were two on and one out when manager Leo Durocher sent Rhodes to pinch-hit for Monte Irvin against Lemon. James Lamar Rhodes had been Durocher's good-luck charm all season, a carefree country boy who didn't play the outfield well enough to be a regular but seemed to hit best under pressure.

The left-handed hitter swung and lifted a soft fly down the right-field line. Avila, drifting back from second base, thought he could catch it. Right fielder Dave Pope seemed to have it lined up. But the high wall angled sharply in the corner, and Pope soon found himself up against it as he neared the line. The ball dropped into the first row of seats, some 260 feet from home plate.

Durocher knew how to play a hot hand. In game 2 he batted Rhodes for Irvin in the fifth inning, and the pinch-hitter's single tied the score, 1–1. Rhodes stayed in the game and later homered in a 3–1 victory.

The Series shifted to Cleveland for game 3, but Rhodes still bedeviled the Indians. His bases-loaded pinch-single in the third inning was the big blow in a 6–2 rout.

Rhodes wasn't needed again as the Giants completed a stunning sweep with a 7–4 fourth-game victory, but never had a part-time player enjoyed a larger role in a Series.

Saved by Billy Boy

The ball hung suspended over the infield for what seemed forever. It was just a pop-up, an easy chance for the first baseman or even the pitcher, if he was interested. And yet, on the uncertain fate of this short fly rested the outcome of a classic seven-game World Series between the New York Yankees and the Brooklyn Dodgers.

The 1952 Series was special for several reasons. Casey Stengel, trying for his fourth world championship in a row as Yankee manager, used his players wisely, coaxing a three-homer performance from 39-year-old first baseman Johnny Mize, who started only four games in the Series. For the Dodgers, center fielder Duke Snider contributed four home runs, tying a Series record, and eight RBI's.

At the other extreme there was Gil Hodges, the strong, silent Brooklyn first baseman. He failed to hit safely in 21 at-bats, yet he had such stature among critical Dodger fans that he was never booed. In fact, a priest in a Brooklyn parish asked his flock to pray for an end to Hodges' slump during the Series.

79

Snider's heroics had lifted the Dodgers to a 6–5, 11-inning victory in game 5 and to within one triumph of their first world championship. But the following day, in Brooklyn's Ebbets Field, Yankee center fielder Mickey Mantle homered in the seventh inning to create a 2–2 tie. Both Dodger runs had been due to Snider homers. The Yankees won, 3–2, on a ground single by pitcher Vic Raschi, which Brooklyn pitcher Billy Loes claimed to have lost in the sun.

The Yankees appeared headed for a routine victory in the seventh game when Mantle homered in the sixth and singled across another run in the seventh for a 4–2 lead. But Stengel's pitching staff was weary from overwork. The Dodgers loaded the bases with one out in the seventh against reliever Raschi, who had worked 7²/₃ innings the day before. Stengel called for Bob Kuzava, a left-hander he saved for just such situations, to face the left-handed-hitting Snider.

The count went to 3-2. The next pitch was high but the eager Snider reached for it and popped out. Jackie Robinson, the fiercest competitor on the Dodgers, was the next batter. Stengel stayed with Kuzava. Again the count went to 3-2. And this time all the base runners took off with the pitch.

The pop by Robinson on the infield grass should

Youngster Mickey Mantle of the Yankees knocked in two runs against the Dodgers in the last game of the 1952 Series.

have been an easy play. But first baseman Joe Collins lost the ball in the sun and Kuzava froze on the mound. The only man with a chance was Billy Martin, the scrappy rookie who played second base, and he was standing almost on the outfield grass. Sensing immediately that no one else was going after the ball, he began a desperate dash.

"I was worried about the wind," he said, "because the prevailing wind at Ebbets Field blew the ball toward home plate. And I was thinking about Yogi [catcher Yogi Berra]. But I heard nothing, no one yelling, no one calling me off the ball."

Martin made a lunging catch at his knees just as the second Dodger runner crossed the plate, preventing a 60-foot double and saving the Series in the bargain. Kuzava, who had closed out the Giants in the sixth game the year before, easily retired the Dodgers in the eighth and ninth innings for the 4–2 victory.

Billy Martin's shoestring catch with bases loaded preserved the Yankees' unbroken chain of championships.

Cookie's Delight

They were not exactly household names. A year later, in fact, not one of them could be found in a major-league box score. But it was Floyd (Bill) Bevens, Cookie Lavagetto, and Al Gionfriddo who made the 1947 World Series between the New York Yankees and the Brooklyn Dodgers such a memorable one.

Bevens was an ordinary pitcher whose luck was as bad as his control. The Yankees led in the Series, two games to one, when first-year manager Bucky Harris chose Bevens, a 7-13 pitcher during the regular season, to start his first and last Series game. Bevens made the experience unforgettable.

Through eight innings the Dodgers were held without a hit. It was not the neatest no-hit bid in history, Bevens having walked eight and allowed a fifth-inning run, but the drama was superb. Bevens retired Bruce Edwards for the first out of the ninth inning but then gave up his ninth walk, to Carl Furillo. The Yankees led, 2–1, and the tying run was on base.

The Dodgers' Al Gionfriddo robs the Yankees' Joe DiMaggio of
a home run in the sixth game of the 1947 World Series.

Gionfriddo, a swift outfielder bought from Pittsburgh early in the season, ran for Furillo. After Johnny Jorgensen fouled out, Gionfriddo boldly stole second base. It was the Dodgers' seventh stolen base of the Series, and the fifth against rookie catcher Yogi Berra. Harris then ordered an intentional walk to dangerous pinch-hitter Pete Reiser, placing the potential winning run on base. Eddie Miksis ran for Reiser.

Eddie Stanky was due up next, but Brooklyn manager Burt Shotton sent up Lavagetto, a 34-year-old part-timer on his way out. The Dodgers had offered Lavagetto a minor-league managing job the previous spring, but he had wanted to play one more year and had spent the season mostly as a pinch-hitter. "So when I went up there to pinch-hit against Bevens," he said, "it was something I had been used to doing all year."

But this situation was unique. He was the last batter between Bevens and the first no-hitter in Series history. On the second pitch from Bevens, the right-handed batter sliced a line drive off Ebbets Field's celebrated right-field wall and both base runners scored easily for a 3–2 Dodger victory. Bevens had become a one-hit loser.

Two days later in game 6 at Yankee Stadium, with the Dodgers holding an 8–5 lead and attempting to even the Series at three games each, Gionfriddo replaced the left fielder to tighten the defense in the sixth inning.

Joe DiMaggio came to bat in the same inning with two on and two out and hit a long drive toward the low bullpen fence in deepest left field. As 74,065 fans, the largest crowd in Series history up to that time, roared in anticipation of a tie score, Gionfriddo ran back, back, back, and, finally, on the warning track, leaped into the air. He speared the ball with his glove hand and held on in spite of smashing into the barrier, preserving an 8–6 victory.

Nonetheless, the Dodgers lost the Series after taking a 2–0 lead in the seventh game. Relief ace Joe Page shut them down on one hit over the last five innings. The key hits in the Yankees' 5–2 victory were a double by Bobby Brown and a single by Tommy Henrich. Bevens was effective in relief, allowing two hits and no runs in 2⅔ innings before turning over the ball to Page.

A Country Run

Enos Slaughter raced around third, past coach Mike Gonzalez's "stop" sign, and into the hearts of America's baseball fans.

The glorious dash gave the hotly contested 1946 World Series between the St. Louis Cardinals and the Boston Red Sox a spectacular finish. And it was one of the great moments in Series history.

This was the Series that brought together the two finest hitters of their generation, Ted Williams of the Red Sox and Stan Musial of the Cards, for the first and last time. Ironically, neither man batted that well. Musial, the National League batting champion with a .365 average, hit only .222 with no home runs and four runs batted in. Williams, the American League's MVP after hitting .342 with 38 home runs in the regular season, batted .200 against a St. Louis shift with no extra-base hits and one run batted in.

With their main sluggers doing poorly, the two teams fought on even terms. The Red Sox won the first, third, and fifth games; the Cards took the second, fourth, and sixth. Cardinal pitcher Harry (The

The Cardinals' Enos Slaughter is safe by a country mile as he scores from first on a single in the seventh game of the 1946 World Series against the Red Sox.

Cat) Brecheen was credited with two complete-game victories in which he allowed a total of one run.

Brecheen, a slight left-hander, was in the bullpen for game 7 as St. Louis moved to a 3–1 lead. But in the top of the eighth inning, pinch-hitters Glen Russell and George Metkovich got hits for Boston and first-year manager Eddie Dyer called for Brecheen. He retired the first two batters but was tagged for a two-run double by Dom DiMaggio.

The game was tied at 3–3 when Enos Slaughter singled off Bob Klinger, leading off the Cards' eighth. He was a true descendant of St. Louis' famous Gashouse Gang, a tough, aggressive player who had the nickname "Country." He now represented the winning run. Slaughter waited impatiently at first as Whitey Kurowski and then Del Rice failed to advance him. The next batter was Harry (The Hat) Walker, the leading hitter of the Series.

When Walker worked the count to 3-2, Slaughter was off and running on the next pitch. The left-handed hitter lined the ball toward left-center, where it was cut off and fumbled by Leon Culberson, who had become the center fielder after Di-Maggio was removed for a pinch-runner. Slaughter had the play in front of him as he rounded second.

"If they hadn't taken DiMaggio out of the game," he said, "I wouldn't have tried to come home, but Culberson didn't have the arm DiMaggio had. I was already at second base when the ball went over the shortstop's head. I figured right then I could score. I never looked at Gonzalez [the third-base coach] and I was told later he put up the 'stop' sign."

Although Culberson recovered quickly in the outfield, shortstop Johnny Pesky had his back to the plate when he took the relay. He never imagined that Slaughter would try to score from first, and he couldn't hear second baseman Bobby Doerr yelling over the noise of the St. Louis crowd. He turned and looked for Slaughter, then hesitated when he saw Slaughter dashing down the third-base line. His throw was late and up the line, and the daring Slaughter slid home safely.

Brecheen then retired the Red Sox in the ninth for his third Series victory. Slaughter, who batted .320, was certified a hero, and Pesky, a fine shortstop, became the goat.

The Missed Third Strike

The batter swung and missed, the game apparently had ended, and a line of policemen swarmed out of the Dodgers' dugout to restrain the jubilant Brooklyn fans. It was the shortest celebration in the history of a franchise that had known few good times.

Perhaps it could have happened only at Ebbets Field, with its rich tradition of wacky events. In 1941 the Dodgers, fresh from their first National League pennant in 21 years, had already suffered one bad break in their first of many World Series meetings with the New York Yankees. It had cost them the third game.

After a split of the first two games at Yankee Stadium, Fat Freddie Fitzsimmons, a 40-year-old veteran of two previous Series with the Giants, had pitched his heart out for the Dodgers in game 3. Locked in a scoreless duel with Yankee left-hander Marius Russo, Fitzsimmons was literally knocked off the mound in the seventh inning when a Russo line drive struck his kneecap and chipped a bone. The Yankees then rattled reliever Hugh Casey for four singles in a row in the eighth inning and scored a 2–1 victory.

What happened next was even more demoralizing. Casey, the Brooklyn relief artist, came back brilliantly the next day in game 4. He took over in the fifth inning, saw his team rally for a 4–3 lead, and held the Yankees scoreless into the ninth. He quickly retired the first two batters and got two strikes on Tommy Henrich, the Yankees' Old Reliable.

Casey's next pitch was a dazzler. On that everyone agreed. The Yankees thought it was a spitball, illegal but still in wide use throughout the majors. Casey and his catcher, Mickey Owen, said it was a hard curve. Whatever it was, Henrich missed it by a foot. And unfortunately Owen did the same.

While the fans leaped to their feet, thinking the Dodgers had evened the Series at two victories apiece, and while the policemen on the field got in everyone's way, Owen chased the pitch to the backstop. Henrich easily reached first on what became the most damaging error in Series history.

Manager Leo Durocher was no less stunned than his pitcher and catcher. For once the Lip was rendered speechless, and he sat still in the dugout as Joe DiMaggio singled, Charlie Keller doubled, Bill Dickey drew a walk, and Joe Gordon doubled. "I was shell-shocked," Durocher said later.

Instead of swallowing a 4–3 defeat, the Yankees emerged with a 7–4 victory. On the following day, in game 5, Ernie Bonham outdueled Whitlow Wyatt, 3–1, and the Yankees were world champions. Owen became the classic Series goat.

"It was all my fault," he said. "It was a great breaking curve and I should have had it. It got away from me, and by the time I got hold of it near the corner of the dugout, I couldn't have thrown anyone out at first."

In their surprise, neither Owen nor Durocher thought to go to the mound and steady Casey. "It was like a punch on the chin," Owen said. "You're stunned. You don't react. I should have gone out to the mound and stalled around a little. It was more my fault than Leo's."

It would remain his fault as long as baseball fans could remember. He would always be Mickey Owen, the man who missed the third strike.

"Me and Paul"

It was the year of the Gashouse Gang. There may have been better teams than the 1934 St. Louis Cardinals, but there was never a brasher, rowdier, more explosive crew than Frankie Frisch's club.

Frisch, who was the second baseman as well as the manager, had gained fame as a battler. So had shortstop Leo Durocher, third baseman Pepper Martin, and outfielder Joe (Ducky) Medwick. The pitching staff didn't lack characters, either. Not with Dizzy Dean, the fast-talking Arkansas hillbilly, around.

The Cardinals had won the National League pennant on the last day of the season, thanks in large measure to Dean. Only 23, Dizzy had won 30 games during the season. His younger brother, Paul, known as Daffy and also a pitcher, had added 19 victories, including a late-season no-hitter against Brooklyn.

Never at a loss for words, although usually at a loss for grammar, Dizzy promised "Me and Paul" would mop up the Series against Detroit. "Leave it

The Dean boys of St. Louis, Dizzy (left) and Daffy, discuss pitching before the 1934 World Series opener against Detroit.

to us," he said. "We'll make pussy cats out of those Tigers."

The elder Dean was as good as his word in the first game, beating Detroit, 8–3, with the help of Medwick's home run and three singles. After a brilliant pitching performance by Lynwood (Schoolboy) Rowe enabled the Tigers to even the Series with a 3–2, 12-inning victory, it was Paul Dean's turn. The 21-year-old was superb in a 4–1 triumph.

In game 4 Dizzy Dean made an unusual entrance and a memorable exit. He was used as a pinch-runner by Frisch in the fourth inning. Standing up while running from first to second on a potential double play, he took shortstop Billy Rogell's throw squarely in the head. Dean had to be carried from the field and taken to a nearby hospital. An examination showed no serious injury. "X-Rays of Dean's Head Show Nothing," was the tongue-in-cheek headline that appeared the following day.

Still, the Cards' situation was no laughing matter. The Tigers won game 4 easily, 10–4, and then bested the dizzy Dizzy in the fifth game, 3–1, behind Tommy Bridges. The last two games would be played in Detroit.

It was Paul Dean to the rescue in the sixth game, outdueling Rowe, 4–3. The light-hitting Durocher had three hits and scored two runs.

That left the Series' outcome up to Dizzy, pitching on just one day's rest, but he was at his best.

The Cards gave Dean a large lead with a seven-run third inning, driving Eldon Auker, Rowe, and Chief Hogsett off the mound before Bridges could cut them off. St. Louis scored two more runs in the sixth and lost a left fielder when Medwick, the Series' leading hitter with a .379 average, slid hard into third baseman Marv Owen, setting off a fight between Medwick and Owen. When Medwick went to his position in the bottom of the inning, the home-town Detroit fans pelted him with fruit, vegetables, and garbage. The disturbance went on for so long that commissioner Kenesaw Mountain Landis finally ordered Medwick out of the game.

Breezing along with an 11–0 lead late in the game, the irrepressible Dean began to experiment with new pitches. The fuming Frisch ordered a pitcher to warm up in the bullpen, whereupon Dean called his manager over. "What's that fella gettin' ready for," Dizzy asked, "openin' day?"

Apparently he was. Dean went the distance, pitching a six-hitter in the 11–0 victory.

The Babe Calls His Shot

The gesture was arrogant and, to most of the spectators who sat in Wrigley Field that October afternoon, unmistakable. Babe Ruth had pointed to the bleachers. He was indicating where his next hit would land, a defiant act by a man who lived by his own rules.

It was 1932 and the final World Series for the Babe and the Yankee team called Murderers' Row. By the time the Yankees again qualified for the Series, in 1936, Ruth had faded from baseball entirely. This would be a kind of going-away party, and Ruth and his teammates made it unforgettable.

The victims were the Chicago Cubs and, as far as the Yankees were concerned, that was fine with them. A feud instantly developed between the teams when the Cubs voted only a half share of their winnings to Mark Koenig, the former Yankee shortstop whose late-season contributions had helped the Cubs win the National League pennant. It also

didn't help the bad feelings that Yankee manager Joe McCarthy had been fired by the Cubs in 1930.

Ruth and the Yankees shouted insults at the Cubs while scoring tremendous victories in the first two games at Yankee Stadium. When the Series continued in Chicago after a day off for travel, Cub fans pelted Ruth and his teammates with lemons. Undaunted, Ruth hit a three-run homer in the first inning. When he came to the plate in the fifth, the score was tied at 4–4.

Now the bench-jockeying from the Chicago bench grew vicious and another lemon rolled toward home plate. Ruth grinned. Then, contemptuously, he stood with his bat on his shoulder as Charlie Root threw two strikes. With the crowd screaming, Ruth held up two fingers to acknowledge the two strikes and then pointed to a spot beyond the right-center-field fence.

Root threw and the Babe connected, driving the ball on a high arc into the bleachers at about the same spot to which he had pointed. The fans were so stunned that they barely acknowledged Lou Gehrig's home run on the next pitch.

The Chicago pitcher later denied that Ruth had called his home run, or else "I'd have knocked him on his fanny with the next pitch, believe me." But Root may have had his back to the plate at the time,

Larrupin' Lou Gehrig of the Yankees smashes a homer against the Cubs in the third game of the 1932 World Series.

The Yankees' Babe Ruth crosses the plate after his first-inning home run in the 1932 opener.

picking up the resin bag. In any event, *The New York Times* reported the next day that "in no mistaken motion the Babe notified the crowd that the nature of his retaliation would be a wallop right out of the confines of the park."

The home run was Ruth's fifteenth and last in Series competition. The Yankees won the third game, 7–5, and they romped, 13–6, in game 4 to complete a Series sweep. Gehrig was the hitting star with three homers and a .529 average, but the 1932 Series would forever be known as the one in which the Babe predicted his final home run.

Wild Horse
of the Osage

He was an odd-looking Bird, this rookie Cardinal with a hawk nose and bandy legs. He called himself Pepper. By the 1931 Series' end, John Leonard Martin had a more celebrated nickname, the Wild Horse of the Osage.

A swift, strong outfielder from Oklahoma who played with an intensity not seen since the prime of Ty Cobb, Martin emerged as a leader of a veteran St. Louis team that featured Frankie Frisch, Jim Bottomley, and Chick Hafey. He was the spark missing the previous year when the Philadelphia Athletics took the Cardinals in six games for their second straight world championship. The A's were back again in 1931, but they weren't prepared for Martin.

It may well have been manager Connie Mack's finest Philadelphia team, and it was his last American League pennant winner. The A's won 107 games, compiled a winning percentage of .704, had a 31-game winner in Lefty Grove, and boasted the

AL batting champion Al Simmons, who hit .390. Against the powerful A's, Martin decided, the Cards' only chance lay in running Philadelphia ragged.

He set about doing just that in the first game, collecting three hits and stealing a base, but the A's won, 6–2, behind Grove.

Martin was more effective in the second game, singling, doubling, stealing two bases, and scoring both runs in a 2–0 St. Louis victory.

He again singled, doubled, and scored two runs as the Cards won the third game, 5–2.

The 3–0 loss to George Earnshaw in game 4 was hardly his fault. He had, naturally, singled and doubled.

So persistent were Martin's efforts that Mack at one point asked Earnshaw, "What's he hitting, George?"

The Philadelphia pitcher was honest. "Everything I throw up to him," Earnshaw replied.

It was the fifth game that fully secured Martin's place in World Series history. That day in Philadelphia, Martin singled twice, homered, and drove in four runs in a 5–1 Card victory. So exasperated was Mickey Cochrane, the A's great catcher, that he asked Martin before one at-bat, "Don't you ever make an out?"

Martin did finally cool off in the last two games. The A's won the sixth game, 8–1, behind Grove and almost came back from a 4–0 deficit in the decisive seventh game, scoring two runs in the ninth and then loading the bases. But the Cards' Wild Bill Hallahan relieved Burleigh Grimes and retired Max Bishop on a fly to center field. Fittingly, it was Martin who caught the final out in the 4–2 St. Louis triumph.

He had staged one of the greatest performances in Series history, collecting 12 hits in 24 at-bats, driving in five runs, scoring five runs, and stealing five bases in six attempts. He drove Cochrane to such distraction on the basepaths that the heavy hitter managed only four singles in 25 at-bats. And he ruined Connie Mack's dream of a third championship in a row, one he would never achieve.

Ol' Pete's Comeback

Grover Cleveland Alexander walked out of the lengthening shadows covering the visitors' bullpen at Yankee Stadium into the glare of the spotlight. Ol' Pete was 39, maybe a little too old for the challenge and maybe a bit shaky from the previous night's celebration. The fate of the 1926 World Series hung on every pitch.

The situation was perilous. The bases were loaded and there were two out in the seventh inning of the seventh game. The St. Louis Cardinals held a 3–2 lead. The Yankee batter was Tony Lazzeri, who had finished second behind teammate Babe Ruth in runs batted in during the regular American League season. Alexander, a midseason buy from the Chicago Cubs where his late hours angered manager Joe McCarthy, had already started and won two games, including a 10–2 decision only the day before. Rogers Hornsby, the Cards' second baseman and manager, looked into Ol' Pete's eyes and handed him the ball.

Once he had been the best pitcher in the National

Grover Cleveland Alexander was a World Series hero at age 39 when he pitched the Cardinals to victory over the Yankees in 1926.

League. Three times he had won 30 games in a season for the Philadelphia Phillies, but his experiences in World War I and increasingly severe epilepsy had driven him to alcoholism. Alexander could still be brilliant once in a while but he wasn't dependable. And this was no time to take a chance.

The Cardinals were in their very first World Series, having edged the Cincinnati Reds by two games to win the NL pennant. For the Yankees, rebounding from a disastrous 1925 season in which they finished seventh, the 1926 season marked the start of a successful era, the first of three straight Series appearances. It was the first year of Murderers' Row, a lineup that intimidated pitchers.

Ruth had enjoyed a great season, batting .372 with 47 homers and 145 RBI's. The fourth game belonged to him as he became the first player to hit three home runs in a Series game. Ruth's first two homers came on successive at-bats against St. Louis starter Flint Rhem. The Yankees' 10–5 victory squared the Series at two games apiece, and when New York pushed across a run in the tenth to beat Bill Sherdel, 3–2, in game 5, the Cards seemed finished.

But Alexander breezed to a 10–2 triumph in the sixth game as Les Bell homered and drove in four runs.

Pop Haines started the seventh game for St. Louis and, after giving up Ruth's fourth home run of the Series, seemed in control until a blister on his finger forced him out of the game in the seventh. Hornsby called for Alexander, who hadn't even warmed up.

"The bullpen in Yankee Stadium is under the bleachers," Alexander said, "and when you're down there you can't see what's going on out on the field. All you know is what you hear from the yells of the fans overhead. So when I came out from under the bleachers, I saw the bases filled and Lazzeri standing in the box. Tony was up there all alone with everyone in that Sunday crowd watching him."

But the fans quickly turned their attention to Alexander. The first pitch was a ball, the second a strike. Then Ol' Pete got a fastball inside and Lazzeri belted it. The runners were racing toward home as the ball hooked foul. Alexander's fourth pitch was a crackling curve, and Lazzeri struck out.

The Yankees went down in order in the eighth. Alexander retired the first two men in the ninth before walking Ruth. With Bob Meusel at the plate, Ruth for some reason tried to steal second and was thrown out, giving the Cardinals a 3–2 victory. The Yankees had lost the World Series and the great Babe Ruth was a bit of a goat.

The Pain of Peckinpaugh

Perhaps the real villain of the 1925 World Series was the weather. Rainy skies and a damp field forced two postponements and caused an unusual number of errors. It was Roger Peckinpaugh's bad luck to be the player most affected.

Peckinpaugh was the star shortstop of the Washington Senators, a pro for 14 seasons, and a veteran of the first Yankee team to win an American League pennant. As much as the great Washington outfielders Sam Rice and Goose Goslin, as much as the immortal Walter Johnson and the Senators' other Hall of Fame pitcher, Stan Coveleski, Peckinpaugh was responsible for the team's second pennant in two years. Maybe more so. The night before the Series against the Pittsburgh Pirates, his fellow players honored him as the league's Most Valuable Player.

But the shortstop had a dismal time in the field as the two teams battled through the first six games. He made one error in the first game, two in the second, one in the third, and one each in the fifth and sixth games. The problem was mostly with his throws. The wet ball slipped out of his hand and skidded in the mud in front of first baseman Joe Judge. Still, thanks to the pitching of Johnson and the hitting of Rice, Goslin, and Joe (Moon) Harris, who had three home runs in the Series, Washington took a three-to-one lead in games.

Until that time no team ever had come back from such a deficit to win a Series. But the Pirates rallied to win the fifth game, 6–3. Pittsburgh evened the Series by edging Washington, 3–2, in the sixth game as Eddie Moore homered, singled, and scored two runs.

After a day's delay the seventh game got under way in a light rain. The gloom was thick at Pittsburgh's Forbes Field, thicker after the Senators jumped to a 4–0 lead in the first inning. The Washington pitcher was Johnson, who had allowed only one run in his two previous starts. But Johnson couldn't control the soggy ball, and the Pirates finally tied the score, 6–6, in the seventh inning.

Peckinpaugh, who had made his seventh error of the Series earlier in the game, still had a chance to be the hero. In the top of the eighth inning he smashed a home run to give Washington a 7–6 lead. There were six Pirate outs to go, and player-manager Bucky Harris decided Johnson was still the man to get them.

The big right-hander retired the first two batters

in the eighth, but then Earl Smith and Carson Bigbee doubled. The score was again tied, 7–7. Eddie Moore drew a walk, but Johnson seemed to have pitched out of trouble when he forced Max Carey, the Pirates' leading hitter in the Series, to hit a pop-up.

Unfortunately Peckinpaugh was the man under the pop-up. He dropped the ball. Kiki Cuyler, the next batter, smacked a double to drive in two runs. Pittsburgh won the game, 9–7, and the Series, and Peckinpaugh set an all-time Series record with eight errors. A more obvious goat never lived.

"The eighth error was the most embarrassing," he said. "It's hard to believe it really happened. It was near the foul line, and I moved over to make the routine catch I had made hundreds of times. When I felt the ball bounce off my glove, I was the most surprised person in the world. I guess I was pressing by then. I must have tried to close my fist too soon."

The Big Train

A nation's good wishes went with Walter Johnson as he walked to the mound in 1924 for his first World Series appearance, a long-cherished dream. The Big Train was 37 and in his eighteenth season as a Washington Senator. For most of that time the Senators were a second-division team against whose mediocrity he had battled valiantly.

The Washington Senators, a standing joke for much of their existence, had somehow edged the Yankees to win the American League pennant by two games. The sparkplug for the team was 28-year-old manager Bucky Harris, who also played second base. Its best hitters were Sam Rice and Goose Goslin, and the pitching staff still revolved around Johnson, who had a 23-7 record in spite of his advanced age.

But the Big Train's fastball had lost some of its steam, and the New York Giants whacked him for 14 hits in taking the first game, 4–3, and 13 more in winning the fifth, 6–2.

It was Tom Zachary, the left-hander who would

The Big Train, Walter Johnson, won the deciding game in the 1924 Series against the Giants.

become famous for serving up Babe Ruth's record sixtieth home run in 1927, who bailed out the Senators with a 2–1 decision, his second victory, in game 6, tying the Series at three games each.

The Giants held a 3–1 lead in the eighth inning of the decisive seventh game when the Senators received the first of three incredible breaks. Harris hit a soft bouncer at Fred Lindstrom, an 18-year-old filling in at third base for the injured Heinie Groh. The ball took a bad hop over his head and two runs scored, tying the score at 3–3.

Harris had used a pinch-hitter for the third Washington pitcher of the game in the eighth. He needed another arm. Who could he turn to but Johnson? "You're the best we've got, Walter," Harris told him. "We've got to win or lose with you."

So the great Johnson, hit hard two days earlier, walked to the mound at Washington's Griffith Stadium. He set down the Giants in the ninth and tenth without a problem, his fastball particularly effective in the fading light. In the eleventh, though, Frankie Frisch led off with a triple. Johnson summoned up the speed that had terrorized a generation of opponents and struck out Ross Youngs and George Kelly, then retired Irish Meusel on a pop fly.

The twelfth was an easy inning, and then came the second of those mystical misfortunes that so often plagued the Giants in the World Series.

With one out in the Washington twelfth, Muddy Ruel lifted a pop foul behind the plate. The Giants'

catcher was Hank Gowdy. Called Old Sarge, Gowdy
was the hero of the 1914 Series when he played for
the "Miracle Braves" and was famous for being the
first major-leaguer to enlist in the army in World
War I. But he failed on his mission this time, stum-
bling on his own discarded mask as the ball dropped
for an error. Given a second chance, Ruel doubled
for only his second hit of the Series.

That brought up Earl McNeely, who hit a
groundball toward Lindstrom. The youngster had
been one of the surprise stars of the Series, collecting four hits off Johnson in the fifth game and playing well at third. But as on Harris' bouncer in the
eighth, the ball struck something hard in front of
him, a pebble maybe, and bounded over his head.
Ruel scored the winning run, and Walter Johnson
had his Series victory, 4–3, in the game that earned
Washington its only championship.

Casey at the Bat

He was a clown in the eyes of many, the man who once took off his cap at home plate to let loose a sparrow. He was a semi-regular nearing the end of a colorful if not glorious playing career. He was Casey Stengel, one of a kind in the history of baseball.

Although his greatest fame would come much later in his years as Yankee manager, in 1923 Stengel used the occasion of the first World Series to be played in New York's new Yankee Stadium to take a few bows. The fact that he was playing for the rival Giants only made his actions stand out more.

Until this year, the Giants and Yankees had both played their games at the Polo Grounds, but Yankee owner Jacob Ruppert had ordered the construction of a new stadium for his team in the Bronx, within sight of the Giants' park. Both teams then won their third pennants in a row, and the Series was scheduled to open in the magnificent new ballpark.

But the hero of the first game turned out to be Stengel. Batting in the ninth inning with the score tied, 4–4, the 33-year-old outfielder lashed a drive

Casey Stengel hit an inside-the-park homer to give the Giants a win over the Yankees in game 1 of the 1923 World Series.

into deepest left-center field between Bob Meusel and Whitey Witt. His run around the bases was hindered by a loose shoe, so he seemed to be limping the last 90 feet before sliding home with an inside-the-park home run.

Before the Series news reports had made much of Stengel's age, but Stengel had the last laugh that day, rising to one knee at home plate and waving bye-bye to Yankee fans.

Shifting to the Polo Grounds for game 2, the Yankees beat the Giants, 4–2, as Ruth homered twice.

But in game 3, the second played at the Stadium, Stengel again stole center stage from the Babe when he homered into the right-field stands for the only run of the game. Since he had been taunted by the Yankees for his "lucky" home run in game 1, Stengel thumbed his nose at the Yankee dugout as he circled the bases. Ruppert protested to commissioner Kenesaw Mountain Landis that Stengel should be disciplined. "When a man hits a home run in a World Series game," Landis replied, "he should be permitted some exuberance—particularly when his name is Casey Stengel."

That was all the fun Stengel and the Giants were to have. The Yankee hitters took command after that in 8–4, 8–1, and 6–4 victories. Bob Meusel had the big hit in the five-run eighth inning that turned the final game and the Series in favor of the Yankees.

Ruth, who had had a terrible Series in 1922,

when he chased a stream of slow curveballs into the dirt, restrained himself this time. He drew eight walks and took advantage of the Giant pitchers' mistakes for three home runs and a .368 average. And the Yankees had won their first world championship.

Still, no one enjoyed a better Series than Stengel, who mugged for the crowd and yet managed to bat .417. Unfortunately, it did not greatly influence his employer, John McGraw, who traded him to Boston after the season. "Maybe I'm lucky," Stengel decided. "If I'd hit three homers, McGraw might have sent me out of the country."

Triple Play

He was a 26-year-old second baseman with a funny-sounding name and a weak bat. He batted only .154 for the Cleveland Indians against the Brooklyn Dodgers in the 1920 World Series. Yet few players have become more identified with baseball's greatest event than Bill Wambsganss.

"Many don't even remember the team I was on, or the position I played, or anything else," he said many years later. What they remembered was his one-of-a-kind play.

This was a best-of-nine Series and the Dodgers had won two of the first three games, which were played at Ebbets Field. Cleveland came back to win the fourth game, played at home, by a 5–1 score. It was the second of spitballer Stan Coveleski's three victories.

Burleigh Grimes started for the Dodgers in the fifth game and fell behind immediately when Elmer Smith hit the first grand slam in Series history for a

4–0 Indian lead. This was to be a game of firsts. In the fourth inning, with two men on base, Cleveland ace Jim Bagby homered off Grimes. No pitcher had ever before hit a home run in a Series.

But the 26,884 fans in Cleveland's League Park hadn't seen anything yet. In the fifth inning, with the Dodgers trailing, 7–0, Pete Kilduff and Otto Miller singled and relief pitcher Clarence Mitchell came to bat with runners on first and second. Manager Wilbert Robinson ordered a hit-and-run play.

Wambsganss was the steadying influence in the infield. His shortstop partner for many years, Ray Chapman, had been killed that summer as the result of a beaning by Yankee pitcher Carl Mays, so the Indians had to go with 21-year-old Joe Sewell, who would make six errors in the Series. The veteran, reacting immediately as he saw the Dodgers break with the pitch, ran to cover second base. It was the perfect move.

Mitchell hit a line drive between Wambsganss and the bag. Wambsganss caught it in full stride and then stepped on second base to easily double-up Kilduff. When he turned to throw the ball to first, he got the surprise of his life. Miller was standing a few feet away, frozen in his tracks, his mouth open.

So Wambsganss took three steps toward first and tagged Miller for the first and only unassisted triple play in Series history. The crowd sat stunned and silent for several moments while figuring out the play, then burst into applause. The Dodgers never fully recovered, losing the game, 8–1. They were shut out by Dusty Mails, 1–0, and Coveleski, 3–0, in the next two games, losing the Series five games to two.

The Black Sox Scandal

The 1919 Series between the Chicago White Sox and the Cincinnati Reds began in a period when baseball was very popular. World War I was over, men were returning home, and the country was moving into an era of prosperity. So great was the postwar enthusiasm for the game, that the championship between the leagues was increased from a best-of-seven to a best-of-nine Series.

Eddie Cicotte, the ace of the favored White Sox, was blown off the mound in the first game as the Reds rolled to an easy 9–1 victory.

Betting on games was common in those days—as it still is—and suddenly the big gamblers shifted their bets to the Reds.

Cincinnati went on to win the Series, five games to three. But there were rumors that several members of the White Sox had accepted bribes to intentionally lose the Series. It wasn't until late in the 1920 season that a Chicago grand jury handed down indictments. Those implicated were Cicotte; pitcher Claude (Lefty) Williams, a three-game loser in the

Series; batting stars Shoeless Joe Jackson and Buck Weaver; as well as Hap Felsch, Chick Gandil, Swede Risberg, and Fred McMullin.

Cicotte, Williams, and Jackson confessed but later took back their confessions. All the players were cleared by a jury. But Kenesaw Mountain Landis, a stern judge who had been selected to serve as baseball's first commissioner partly as a result of the fix rumors, banned the eight from organized baseball for life. In this way the integrity of the game was preserved, but the 1919 Series became forevermore known as the Black Sox scandal.

The course of events took much of the glory away from the Reds, who steadfastly believed they had beaten the White Sox fair and square. They pointed to the .375 and .324 batting averages of Chicago's Jackson and Weaver, the fact that Cicotte came back to win the sixth game, and the .214 average of National League batting champion Edd Roush against the Chicago pitchers.

A man who gained in stature as a result of the disclosures was pitcher Dickie Kerr, the White Sox's little left-hander. He twice beat the Reds, 3–0 and 5–4, and to his dying day he was honored as an honest man.

But many a boy's belief in baseball was shattered by the gambling charges. As it was for the youngster who met Joe Jackson on the courthouse steps and told him, "Say it ain't so, Joe."

126

The Miracle Braves

They were calling the Philadelphia Athletics baseball's first dynasty. "Break up the A's," grumbled fans and not a few baseball people.

"The A's," said John McGraw, ruler of the New York Giants, "have become a menace to the World Series and to my league."

Indeed, Connie Mack's A's had defeated National League teams in three of the four previous Series, and Philadelphia's proud team was heavily favored to squash the Boston Braves in 1914 and win another championship. There were those, in fact, who considered it an embarrassment to the NL for the Braves to appear on the same field with the A's.

Among this group was Charles Albert (Chief) Bender, the great Philadelphia right-hander. He was sent to New York to scout the Braves in the final week of the season. Manager Mack wanted him to find weaknesses in the team that the A's could take advantage of in the Series. But Bender went fishing instead. When Mack confronted him, Bender replied, "We don't need to scout this bush-league outfit."

From all appearances that's what the Braves were. They were a collection of discards made into a team by manager George Stallings, a team that had been in last place in mid-July. But the Braves then won 34 of their next 44 games to climb past the Giants and into first place in September. They finished at the top of the league by a staggering 10½ games.

Still, the Braves were considered a lost cause against the A's, especially when third baseman Red Smith, one of their best hitters, broke a leg virtually on the night before the first game of the Series. That left Boston with only three everyday players and one .300 hitter in the lineup. Philadelphia had its famed $100,000 infield and the most effective pitching staff in baseball.

Fittingly, Bender was given the starting assignment for the A's in the first game. But he was driven out of the box in the sixth inning, the first time he had failed to complete a Series game. The Braves won, 7–1, as Hank Gowdy, a catcher whom the Giants had sold three years earlier, singled, doubled, and tripled in three at-bats. "Pretty good hitting for a bush-league team, isn't it?" Mack needled Bender after the game.

Bill James of the Braves outdueled Eddie Plank, 1–0, in the second game and pitched two innings of hitless relief two days later in a 5–4, 12-inning victory when the Series continued in Boston's Fenway Park, which the Red Sox had lent to the Braves for the occasion. Gowdy, who had homered and doubled earlier in the third game, doubled again in the twelfth inning. A pinch-runner, Les Mann, scored the winning run on a throwing error by pitcher Bullet Joe Bush.

Dick Rudolph, who had won the first game for the Braves, wrapped up the Series with a 3–1 victory assisted by second baseman Johnny Evers' two RBI's. Not only were the A's beaten but they were eliminated in four games, the first team to be swept in Series history.

Gowdy, a .243 hitter during the regular season, became a real hero, the first player to bat over .500 in a Series. He finished at .545 and his six hits included a homer, a triple, and three doubles. He also drew five walks. "My regret," manager Mack said, "is that I didn't walk him oftener."

While Rudolph and Gowdy went on to do a night-club comedy act for $1,500 a week, Mack set about restructuring his team. He believed many of his players were concentrating more on offers from the rival Federal League than on winning the Series. Bender and Plank did jump to the third league, and Mack sold Eddie Collins, Home Run Baker, and Jack Coombs to rival AL clubs, breaking up the A's after all.

Snodgrass' Muff

The man was a thoroughly reliable outfielder, at times even brilliant, and one of the mainstays of John McGraw's New York Giants. But Fred Snodgrass' fame in the 1912 World Series was due to a play he did not make.

It was an outstanding Giant team that faced the Boston Red Sox in the Series. Beaten by the Philadelphia A's in the Series the year before, the Giants had rebounded to win 103 games in 1912, finishing 10 games ahead of the second-place Pittsburgh Pirates in the National League race.

The Red Sox, with 34-game-winner Smokey Joe Wood winning both his starts, took a 3–1 lead in games—but the Giants battled back. The fifth game ended in a tie and was credited to neither team. The Giants won the sixth game, 5–2, behind Rube Marquard, and battered Wood, 11–4, in game 7. At that point each team had won three games.

Christy Mathewson was the starting pitcher for the Giants in the decisive game. If he was no longer the superstar he had been in the first decade of the century, he was still the pitcher most respected by teammates and opponents alike. Matty had won 23 games in 1912, the tenth season in a row that he posted 20 or more victories, and he was as dependable an athlete as ever lived.

For six innings Mathewson held the Red Sox scoreless. He carried a 1–0 lead into the seventh, a lead that would have been larger if Harry Hooper hadn't made a great catch on Larry Doyle's long drive in the fifth. In the seventh, though, Mathewson gave up the tying run on Olaf Henriksen's double. Henriksen was batting for Boston starter Hugh Bedient, who was replaced on the mound by Wood, the Red Sox ace.

When the Giants scored a run off Wood in the top of the tenth, they appeared certain winners. But pinch-hitter Clyde Engle led off the Boston half of the inning with a lazy fly into left-center field. Snodgrass, the center fielder, called left fielder Red Murray off the ball and reached to catch it. He failed. The ball trickled out of his glove and fell to the ground. Engle reached second on the error.

In his own mind Snodgrass made up for the misplay when he made a brilliant, over-the-shoulder grab of Hooper's next drive. But the public would always remember him as a goat because of what followed. After Steve Yerkes drew a walk, Tris Speaker hit a foul pop near the first-base coaching box. Fred Merkle, the first baseman whose base-running boner had cost the Giants a pennant four years earlier, somehow never moved. Catcher Chief Myers couldn't get to the ball, which dropped foul.

On the very next pitch Speaker, a .383 hitter during the American League season, singled sharply, driving in the tying run and sending Yerkes to third. When Larry Gardner followed with a long fly, Yerkes scored the Series-winning run in the 2–1 game.

Somehow Merkle's daydreaming at first got less attention than Snodgrass' error. But McGraw knew the score. He was one of the few people who said he did not blame the loss of the Series on Snodgrass. In fact, he raised the outfielder's salary $1,000 for the 1913 season. The tough-talking Giants' manager firmly believed that although errors are part of baseball, he could not tolerate those that were mistakes of judgment.

"I don't blame Snodgrass," McGraw said. "It's something that's likely to happen to any outfielder now and then. There is no excuse, however, for Merkle not catching Speaker's ball."

Home Run Baker

It was the era of the dead ball, and teams scraped for runs. They bunted, they played hit-and-run, and they stole bases because few men in baseball were able to hit the heavy ball out of the park. That's what made Frank Baker's talent so special.

Baker was the third baseman on the Philadelphia Athletics, a member of Connie Mack's justly famous $100,000 infield. In 1911 he led the American League in home runs with nine. It was the first of four home-run championships in a row he would win, never hitting more than 12 in a season.

But what gained him his reputation as a great slugger, what earned him the nickname Home Run Baker, what established him as a player worthy of the Hall of Fame, was his performance against the New York Giants in the 1911 World Series. In a re-match of the great rivals in the 1905 Series, in a widely anticipated showdown between the two most famous teams of the era, Baker's power proved a mightier weapon than the Giants' strategy.

The Giants were a crafty and resourceful team

The Athletics' Frank (Home Run) Baker knocked in seven runs against the Giants in the 1911 World Series.

that had stolen 347 bases during the regular season. A pitching staff led by the great Christy Mathewson and featuring brilliant southpaw Rube Marquard didn't need many runs. What runs the Giants made, they often stole.

Typically, the Giants won the opener at the Polo Grounds, 2–1, behind Mathewson, in spite of collecting only five hits. In the second game, however, with the score tied at 1–1, Baker hit a two-run homer off Marquard for a 3–1 Philadelphia victory that evened the Series at a game apiece.

Two newspaper chains were paying Mathewson and Marquard to write daily columns on the Series under their names. Following game 2, the ghost-written story under Matty's name criticized Marquard for pitching "carelessly" to Baker.

That turned out to be very embarrassing to Mathewson the following day when Baker homered against him in the ninth inning. That tied the score, 1–1, and the third game went into extra innings. The A's won, 3–2, in 11 innings, with Jack Coombs gaining credit for the shocking victory. Marquard's column promptly speculated that perhaps Matty had also been "careless."

A full week of rain intervened before Matty was beaten by the A's Chief Bender, 4–2, in game 4 as Baker doubled twice, drove in one run, and scored another.

The Giants rallied for two runs in the ninth inning of game 5 to tie the score and achieved a 4–3

135

victory in the tenth to keep their Series hopes alive.

But the A's shelled Leon Ames, George Wiltse, and Marquard, 13–2, in the sixth game, getting revenge for their five-game loss in 1905.

The Giants' running game was never a factor in the Series. They stole only four bases in the six games, the same number stolen by the A's, and had four men thrown out in a single game. Meanwhile, the A's out-homered the Giants, 3–0, and Home Run Baker became a national hero and acquired a famous nickname.

The Rookie Who Tamed the Tigers

Among them, Howie Camnitz, Vic Willis, and Al Leifield had won 66 games in the 1909 season, a season in which the Pittsburgh Pirates had won 110 games and the National League pennant. Among them, in the World Series against the Detroit Tigers, those same players had won no games. Enter Charles (Babe) Adams.

Adams was a 27-year-old rookie pitcher who had won 12 games for the Pirates while pitching mostly against the weaker National League teams. He was a chubby-cheeked Missouri farmboy who relied on a curveball, a pitch that gave the Tigers trouble. Adams also never drank alcohol, which pleased manager Fred Clarke. His top pitcher, 25-game-winner Camnitz, drank more than his share and was in no condition to start the Series opener at shiny new Forbes Field in Pittsburgh.

About an hour before the first game Clarke told the rookie he would throw the first pitch of the Se-

137

ries. "Then I handed him a new ball and his hands started to shake so much he almost dropped it," Clarke said. "I gave him a look of contempt and said, 'What's the matter, kid, you yellow?' "

It was part of Clarke's psychology to make Adams so mad at him that he wouldn't be nervous at the prospect of facing the great Ty Cobb, Wahoo Sam Crawford, and the other heavy hitters on the Tigers. And it worked. After allowing a first-inning run, he held Detroit scoreless the rest of the way as Pittsburgh won, 4–1.

Camnitz was available for the second game but he had a dreadful day. Blessed with a 2–0 lead in the first inning, he soon lost it, his poise, and the game. The Tigers scored two in the second inning and three in the third, the last crossing the plate on Cobb's daring steal of home, in a 7–2 triumph.

This Series marked the first match of titans, Cobb against the Pirates' Honus Wagner. They were the batting champions of their leagues, future Hall of Famers who were destined never to play in another Series. Perhaps influenced by Cobb, Wagner had three hits, stole three bases, and drove in three runs as Pittsburgh won game 3 by an 8–6 score.

Leifield got the call in the fourth game and was ineffective in a 5–0 loss.

With the Series at two games apiece, Clarke went back to Adams, and although he had a rougher trip, the rookie went the distance in an 8–4 victory. A two-run homer by Clarke, who was also the Pirates' regular left fielder, was the big blow.

The Tigers hung on to beat Pittsburgh, 5–4, in the sixth game, sending the Series to the seven-game limit for the first time. Clarke, who wanted his players relaxed, invited them to a party in his hotel room the night before the game. He provided the beer, a barbershop quartet, and comedians.

It didn't hurt Pittsburgh's cause that Adams was pitching the seventh game. Working on only two days' rest, Adams pitched a masterful six-hitter. He held Cobb and Crawford hitless in four appearances apiece (Cobb managed only one hit off Adams in 11 at-bats) and breezed to an 8–0 victory as Wagner and Dots Miller each drove in two runs.

Wagner, 35, enjoyed an outstanding Series, batting .333 and accounting for six of the 18 steals against catcher Charlie Schmidt. The 22-year-old Cobb, perhaps the greatest hitter in baseball history, batted only .231 and emerged a Series loser for the third time in three years.

Big Six

He was that rare athlete who upgraded not just his team but his sport by his presence. Before his arrival at the turn of the century, professional baseball was a game played by roughnecks, uneducated farmboys, and city scrappers who chewed tobacco and didn't know which fork (if any) to use at dinner. Or so they were thought of by the public.

Christy Mathewson changed that. Matty lent the sport respectability. He was a college man, from Bucknell, at a time when few players had made it through high school. He was tall and handsome, well-mannered and articulate. He was the first golden boy of baseball. Big Six, he was called, because of his size.

And the 1905 World Series was his stage. It was the first official championship of the National and American leagues. Two years earlier the pennant winners from both leagues had met by mutual consent of the competing teams—the Boston Red Sox and the Pittsburgh Pirates. John McGraw, the famed manager of the New York Giants, had re-

140

Christy Mathewson of the Giants hurled three shutouts against the A's in the 1905 World Series.

jected a second Series in 1904, however, while his team was in the process of winning the NL flag.

McGraw branded the AL a "minor league." It just so happened the New York Highlanders (the forerunners of the Yankees) were leading the "minor league" at the time, and the lordly Giants were in no hurry to grant equal status to their new rivals.

By the time the Giants had clinched their second straight pennant in 1905, the Series was a fixture of baseball. Under rules drawn up by Giants' president John T. Brush and approved by the three-man National Commission, the NL and AL champions were to meet in a seven-game Series, and the profits would be distributed among the players, the owners, and the commission.

The Philadelphia Athletics, managed by Connie Mack, won the AL pennant, bringing together the two most famous personalities in baseball for the first time. For the stiff-necked Mack, it was to be the first of eight World Series appearances; for the fiery McGraw, the first of nine.

The Athletics suffered a crippling blow even before the Series began. Rube Waddell, the ace left-hander who had won 27 games and struck out 286 batters, was ruled out of the Series with a shoulder injury. The fun-loving Waddell had suffered the injury while roughhousing with a teammate.

Mack never got to match Waddell against Mathewson, and Matty stole the show. This was Matty's fifth full year in the majors and the third season in a row that he had won 30 or more games. Throwing his famous fadeaway, which later generations would call a screwball, Matty won 31 games, struck out 208 batters, and compiled an earned-run average of 1.27, all NL bests.

McGraw outfitted the Giants in special uniforms of black flannel with white trim, which the superstitious manager insisted gave his team a psychological advantage. But the greatest advantage enjoyed by the Giants was the presence of Matty on the mound. Every game in the five-game Series was decided by shutout, and Matty was responsible for three of them. It's a record that has never been equaled.

Mathewson allowed a total of 14 hits in 3–0, 9–0, and 2–0 victories in a span of six days. He walked only one batter and struck out 18. As his Hall of Fame plaque would read many years later: "Matty was the Master of them all."

WORLD SERIES RESULTS

Year	AL Champion	NL Champion	World Series Winner
1903	Boston Red Sox	Pittsburgh Pirates	Boston, 5–3
1904	*There was no World Series.*		
1905	Philadelphia Athletics	New York Giants	New York, 4–1
1906	Chicago White Sox	Chicago Cubs	Chicago (AL), 4–2
1907	Detroit Tigers	Chicago Cubs	Chicago 4–0–1*
1908	Detroit Tigers	Chicago Cubs	Chicago, 4–1
1909	Detroit Tigers	Pittsburgh Pirates	Pittsburgh, 4–3
1910	Philadelphia Athletics	Chicago Cubs	Philadelphia, 4–1
1911	Philadelphia Athletics	New York Giants	Philadelphia, 4–2
1912	Boston Red Sox	New York Giants	Boston, 4–3–1*
1913	Philadelphia Athletics	New York Giants	Philadelphia, 4–1
1914	Philadelphia Athletics	Boston Braves	Boston, 4–0
1915	Boston Red Sox	Philadelphia Phillies	Boston, 4–1
1916	Boston Red Sox	Brooklyn Dodgers	Boston, 4–1
1917	Chicago White Sox	New York Giants	Chicago, 4–2
1918	Boston Red Sox	Chicago Cubs	Boston, 4–2
1919	Chicago White Sox	Cincinnati Reds	Cincinnati, 5–2
1920	Cleveland Indians	Brooklyn Dodgers	Cleveland, 5–2
1921	New York Yankees	New York Giants	New York (NL), 5–3
1922	New York Yankees	New York Giants	New York (NL), 4–0–1*
1923	New York Yankees	New York Giants	New York (AL), 4–2
1924	Washington Senators	New York Giants	Washington, 4–2
1925	Washington Senators	Pittsburgh Pirates	Pittsburgh, 4–3
1926	New York Yankees	St. Louis Cardinals	St. Louis, 4–3
1927	New York Yankees	Pittsburgh Pirates	New York, 4–0
1928	New York Yankees	St. Louis Cardinals	New York, 4–0
1929	Philadelphia Athletics	Chicago Cubs	Philadelphia, 4–2
1930	Philadelphia Athletics	St. Louis Cardinals	Philadelphia, 4–2
1931	Philadelphia Athletics	St. Louis Cardinals	St. Louis, 4–3
1932	New York Yankees	Chicago Cubs	New York, 4–0
1933	Washington Senators	New York Giants	New York, 4–1
1934	Detroit Tigers	St. Louis Cardinals	St. Louis, 4–3
1935	Detroit Tigers	Chicago Cubs	Detroit, 4–2
1936	New York Yankees	New York Giants	New York (AL), 4–2
1937	New York Yankees	New York Giants	New York (AL), 4–1

* *The third number stands for tie games.*

145

1938	New York Yankees	Chicago Cubs	New York, 4–0
1939	New York Yankees	Cincinnati Reds	New York, 4–0
1940	Detroit Tigers	Cincinnati Reds	Cincinnati, 4–3
1941	New York Yankees	Brooklyn Dodgers	New York, 4–1
1942	New York Yankees	St. Louis Cardinals	St. Louis, 4–1
1943	New York Yankees	St. Louis Cardinals	New York, 4–1
1944	St. Louis Browns	St. Louis Cardinals	St. Louis (NL), 4–2
1945	Detroit Tigers	Chicago Cubs	Detroit, 4–3
1946	Boston Red Sox	St. Louis Cardinals	St. Louis, 4–3
1947	New York Yankees	Brooklyn Dodgers	New York, 4–3
1948	Cleveland Indians	Boston Braves	Cleveland, 4–2
1949	New York Yankees	Brooklyn Dodgers	New York, 4–1
1950	New York Yankees	Philadelphia Phillies	New York, 4–0
1951	New York Yankees	New York Giants	New York (AL), 4–2
1952	New York Yankees	Brooklyn Dodgers	New York, 4–3
1953	New York Yankees	Brooklyn Dodgers	New York, 4–2
1954	Cleveland Indians	New York Giants	New York, 4–0
1955	New York Yankees	Brooklyn Dodgers	Brooklyn, 4–3
1956	New York Yankees	Brooklyn Dodgers	New York, 4–3
1957	New York Yankees	Milwaukee Braves	Milwaukee, 4–3
1958	New York Yankees	Milwaukee Braves	New York, 4–3
1959	Chicago White Sox	Los Angeles Dodgers	Los Angeles, 4–2
1960	New York Yankees	Pittsburgh Pirates	Pittsburgh, 4–3
1961	New York Yankees	Cincinnati Reds	New York, 4–1
1962	New York Yankees	San Francisco Giants	New York, 4–3
1963	New York Yankees	Los Angeles Dodgers	Los Angeles, 4–0
1964	New York Yankees	St. Louis Cardinals	St. Louis, 4–3
1965	Minnesota Twins	Los Angeles Dodgers	Los Angeles, 4–3
1966	Baltimore Orioles	Los Angeles Dodgers	Baltimore, 4–0
1967	Boston Red Sox	St. Louis Cardinals	St. Louis, 4–3
1968	Detroit Tigers	St. Louis Cardinals	Detroit, 4–3
1969	Baltimore Orioles	New York Mets	New York, 4–1
1970	Baltimore Orioles	Cincinnati Reds	Baltimore, 4–1
1971	Baltimore Orioles	Pittsburgh Pirates	Pittsburgh, 4–3
1972	Oakland A's	Cincinnati Reds	Oakland, 4–3
1973	Oakland A's	New York Mets	Oakland, 4–3
1974	Oakland A's	Los Angeles Dodgers	Oakland, 4–1
1975	Boston Red Sox	Cincinnati Reds	Cincinnati, 4–3
1976	New York Yankees	Cincinnati Reds	Cincinnati, 4–0
1977	New York Yankees	Los Angeles Dodgers	New York, 4–2
1978	New York Yankees	Los Angeles Dodgers	New York, 4–2
1979	Baltimore Orioles	Pittsburgh Pirates	Pittsburgh, 4–3
1980	Kansas City Royals	Philadelphia Phillies	Philadelphia, 4–2
1981	New York Yankees	Los Angeles Dodgers	Los Angeles, 4–2

ABOUT THE AUTHOR

Joe Gergen, sports columnist for *Newsday* (Long Island, New York), has covered the World Series since 1963. He is the author of two previous books—*Dr. J: The Story of Julius Erving* and *Roger Staubach of the Dallas Cowboys*—and has contributed to *Sport, Inside Sports,* and *The Sporting News*. In 1971 he won the National Headliners' Club Award for outstanding sports journalism. Gergen, a graduate of Boston College, was a sportswriter at United Press International before joining *Newsday* in 1968.